Austerity
Motoring
From Armistice until the mid-Fifties

Malcolm Bobbitt

VELOCE PUBLISHING
THE PUBLISHER OF FINE AUTOMOTIVE BOOKS

Also from Veloce Publishing:

SpeedPro Series
4-Cylinder Engine - How to Blueprint & Build a Short Block for High Performance by Des Hammill
Alfa Romeo Twin Cam Engines - How to Power Tune by Jim Kartalamakis
BMC 998cc A-Series Engine - How to Power Tune by Des Hammill
BMC/Rover 1275cc A-Series Engines - How to Power Tune by Des Hammill
Camshafts - How to Choose & Time them for Maximum Power by Des Hammill
Cylinder Heads - How to Build, Modify & Power Tune Second Edition by Peter Burgess
Distributor-type Ignition Systems - How to Build & Power Tune by Des Hammill
Fast Road Car - How to Plan and Build by Daniel Stapleton
Ford SOHC 'Pinto' & Sierra Cosworth DOHC Engines - How to Power Tune Updated & Revised Edition by Des Hammill
Ford V8 - How to Power Tune Small Block Engines by Des Hammill
Harley-Davidson Evolution Engines - How to Build & Power Tune by Des Hammill
Holley Carburetors - How to Build & Power Tune by Des Hammill
Jaguar XK Engines - How to Power Tune by Des Hammill
MG Midget & Austin-Healey Sprite - How to Power Tune Updated Edition by Daniel Stapleton
MGB 4-Cylinder Engine - How to Power Tune by Peter Burgess
MGB - How to Give your MGB V8 Power Updated & Revised Edition by Roger Williams
MGB, MGC & MGB V8 - How to Improve by Roger Williams
Mini Engines - How to Power Tune on a Small Budget by Des Hammill
Motorsport - Getting Started in by Sam Collins
Rover V8 Engines - How to Power Tune by Des Hammill
Sportscar/Kitcar Suspension & Brakes - How to Build & Modify by Des Hammill
SU Carburettors - How to Build & Modify for High Performance by Des Hammill
Tiger Avon Sportscar - How to Build Your Own by Jim Dudley
TR2, 3 & TR4 - How to Improve by Roger Williams
TR5, 250 & TR6 - How to Improve by Roger Williams
V8 Engine - How to Build a Short Block for High Performance by Des Hammill
Volkswagen Beetle Suspension, Brakes & Chassis - How to Modify for High Performance by James Hale
Volkswagen Bus Suspension, Brakes & Chassis - How to Modify for High Performance by James Hale
Weber DCOE, & Dellorto DHLA Carburetors - How to Build & Power Tune Third Edition by Des Hammill

Colour Family Album Series
Alfa Romeo by Andrea & David Sparrow
Bubblecars & Microcars by Andrea & David Sparrow
Bubblecars & Microcars, More by Andrea & David Sparrow
Citroen 2CV by Andrea & David Sparrow
Citroen DS by Andrea & David Sparrow
Custom VWs by Andrea & David Sparrow
Fiat & Abarth 500 & 600 by Andrea & David Sparrow
Lambretta by Andrea & David Sparrow
Mini & Mini Cooper by Andrea & David Sparrow
Motor Scooters by Andrea & David Sparrow
Porsche by Andrea & David Sparrow
Triumph Sportscars by Andrea & David Sparrow
Vespa by Andrea & David Sparrow
VW Beetle by Andrea & David Sparrow
VW Bus, Camper, Van & Pick-up by Andrea & David Sparrow
VW Custom Beetle by Andrea & David Sparrow

General
AC Two-litre Saloons & Buckand Sportscars by Leo Archibald
Alfa Romeo Berlinas (Saloons/Sedans) by John Tipler
Alfa Romeo Giulia Coupe GT & GTA by John Tipler
Anatomy of the Works Minis by Brian Moylan
Automotive A-Z, Lane's Dictionary of Automotive Terms by Keith Lane
Automotive Mascots by David Kay & Lynda Springate
Bentley Continental, Corniche and Azure, by Martin Bennett
BMW 5-Series by Marc Cranswick
BMW Z-Cars by James Taylor
British Cars, The Complete Catalogue of, 1895-1975 by Culshaw & Horrobin
British Police Cars by Nick Walker
Caravans, The Illustrated History 1919-1959 by Andrew Jenkinson
Caravans, The Illustrated History from 1960 by Andrew Jenkinson
Bugatti Type 40 by Barrie Price
Bugatti 46/50 Updated Edition by Barrie Price

Bugatti 57 2nd Edition - by Barrie Price
Caravanning & Trailer Tenting, the Essential Handbook by Len Archer
Chrysler 300 - America's Most Powerful Car by Robert Ackerson
Cobra - The Real Thing! by Trevor Legate
Cortina - Ford's Bestseller by Graham Robson
Coventry Climax Racing Engines by Des Hammill
Daimler SP250 'Dart' by Brian Long
Datsun/Nissan 280ZX & 300ZX by Brian Long
Datsun Z - From Fairlady to 280Z by Brian Long
Dune Buggy Handbook by James Hale
Dune Buggies by James Hale
Fiat & Abarth 124 Spider & Coupe by John Tipler
Fiat & Abarth 500 & 600 Second edition by Malcolm Bobbitt
Ford F100/F150 Pick-up by Robert Ackerson
Ford GT40 by Trevor Legate
Ford Model Y by Sam Roberts
Harley-Davidson, Growing up by Jean Davidson
Jaguar XJ-S, by Brian Long
Karmann-Ghia Coupe & Convertible by Malcolm Bobbitt
Land Rover, The Half-Ton Military by Mark Cook
Lea-Francis Story, The by Barrie Price
Lexus Story, The by Brian Long
Lola - The Illustrated History (1957-1977) by John Starkey
Lola - All The Sports Racing & Single-Seater Racing Cars 1978-1997 by John Starkey
Lola T70 - The Racing History & Individual Chassis Record 3rd Edition by John Starkey
Lotus 49 by Michael Oliver
Mazda MX-5/Miata 1.6 Enthusiast's Workshop Manual by Rod Grainger & Pete Shoemark
Mazda MX-5/Miata 1.8 Enthusiast's Workshop Manual by Rod Grainger & Pete Shoemark
Mazda MX-5 (& Eunos Roadster) - The World's Favourite Sportscar by Brian Long
MGA by John Price Williams
MGB & MGB GT - Expert Guide (Auto-Doc Series) by Roger Williams
Mini Cooper - The Real Thing! by John Tipler
Mitsubishi Lancer Evo by Brian Long
Motor Racing at Goodwood in the Sixties by Tony Gardiner
Motorhomes, The Illustrated History by Andrew Jenkinson
MR2 - Toyota's Mid-engined Sports Car by Brian Long
Pontiac Firebird by Marc Cranswick
Porsche 356 by Brian Long
Porsche 911R, RS & RSR, 4th Ed. by John Starkey
Porsche 911 - The Definitive History 1963-1971 by Brian Long
Porsche 911 - The Definitive History 1971-1977 by Brian Long
Porsche 911 - The Definitive History 1977-1987 by Brian Long
Porsche 911 - The Definitive History 1987-1997 by Brian Long
Porsche 914 & 914-6 by Brian Long
Porsche 924 by Brian Long
Porsche 944 by Brian Long
Rolls-Royce Silver Shadow/Bentley T Series Corniche & Camargue Updated Edition by Malcolm Bobbitt
Rolls-Royce Silver Spirit, Silver Spur & Bentley Mulsanne by Malcolm Bobbitt
Rolls-Royce Silver Wraith, Dawn & Cloud/Bentley MkVI, R & S Series by Martyn Nutland
RX-7 - Mazda's Rotary Engine Sportscar by Brian Long
Singer Story: Cars, Commercial Vehicles, Bicycles & Motorcycles by Kevin Atkinson
Subaru Impreza by Brian Long
Taxi! The Story of the 'London' Taxicab by Malcolm Bobbitt
Three Wheelers by Malcolm Bobbitt
Triumph Motorcycles & the Meriden Factory by Hughie Hancox
Triumph Tiger Cub Bible by Mike Estall
Triumph Trophy Bible by Harry Woolridge
Triumph TR2/3/3A, How to Restore, by Roger Williams
Triumph TR4/4A, How to Restore, by Roger Williams
Triumph TR5/250 & 6, How to Restore, by Roger Williams
Triumph TR6 by William Kimberley
Turner's Triumphs, Edward Turner & his Triumph Motorcycles by Jeff Clew
Velocette Motorcycles - MSS to Thruxton by Rod Burris
Volkswagens of the World by Simon Glen
VW Beetle Cabriolet by Malcolm Bobbitt
VW Beetle - The Car of the 20th Century by Richard Copping
VW Bus, Camper, Van, Pickup by Malcolm Bobbitt
Works Rally Mechanic by Brian Moylan

First published in 2003 by Veloce Publishing Limited, 33 Trinity Street, Dorchester DT1 1TT, England.
Fax 01305 268864/e-mail info@veloce.co.uk/web www.veloce.co.uk or www.velocebooks.com
ISBN 1-903706-86-6/UPC 36847-00286-2

Readers with ideas for automotive books, or books on other transport or related hobby subjects, are invited to write to the editorial director of Veloce Publishing at the above address.
British Library Cataloguing in Publication Data - A catalogue record for this book is available from the British Library.

Typesetting (URW Imperial T), design and page make-up all by Veloce Publishing Ltd on Apple Mac. Printed in Croatia.

Contents

Introduction 5
In Time of War 7
Export or Die..20
Keeping Going 32

A New Car? 47
Luxury and Speed in Austerity ... 72
Index 95

Acknowledgements

My grateful thanks are extended to Tim Wright of LAT Photographic for supplying a number of photographs, also to Martin Bourne, Colin Chipperfield, Graham Hull, Elaine Williamson, Metropolitan Police Museum, Rolls-Royce, the Sir Henry Royce Memorial Foundation, and the librarians at the National Motor Museum. Andrew Minney kindly read my manuscript and I appreciate his comments and helpful advice. Finally, my thanks to my wife Jean who has tolerated the process of me compiling yet another book with her usual patience.

A number of images used in this book are from my own collection and whilst I have endeavoured to trace their origins this has sometimes been difficult, and I therefore apologise if I have failed to give the appropriate credit.

The involvement of the motor industry to produce aero engines for the armed services led to the establishment of shadow factories around the country. Here is the scene at Pyms Lane, Crewe, around 1936 when the Rolls-Royce works were under construction. 28,000 Merlin and Griffon engines were built here out of a total of more than 150,000 worldwide. (Rolls-Royce).

The distribution of gas masks during the lead up to the Second World War was a precaution against the threat of chemical attack. Gas masks were issued in 1938, after which gas attack drills were conducted around the country. In June 1941 Londoners were subjected to mock gas assaults to make people aware of the dangers that existed, and what should be done in case of emergency. In August 1941 *The Autocar* carried a feature explaining how cars and motorists would be affected in the event of a gas alert, and while the piece was informative and offered practical advice, it made for some disturbing reading. (LAT Photographic)

Introduction

In writing this book I have allowed myself to indulge on a journey back through time to a period, from the outbreak of war in 1939 to the mid-1950s, that was ravaged by conflict, the aftermath of which many endured in hardship and misery.

Life carried on with most people trying to live as normal a life as circumstances allowed, despite hostilities and the shortages in food and raw materials. The population, not least doctors, farmers, industrial workers and those in the commercial and public sectors, largely relied on the motor vehicle in one way or another, often at the mercy of air raids, blackouts and grim conditions. Reliance upon motor vehicles was at no time greater, whether as fighting machines or a means of conveying essential supplies, not to mention getting people to and from work, to railway stations, ports or airfields.

Never was oil such a precious commodity, for without it the war effort would have been gravely compromised. To maximise its resourcefulness rationing was an obvious necessity, even if it did mean loss of personal independence. Fuel supplies were made available to essential users, but for many motorists there was no alternative but to either lay up their cars or dispense with them entirely. Innovation played its part when a number of motorists invested in gas-producers to enable them to run their vehicles on alternative fuels. In London and other big cities cars running with gasbags precariously mounted on their roofs were a familiar sight.

Post-war austerity saw the motor industry aiding Britain's financial recovery. Despite the deficiencies in raw materials, a vigorous export drive despatched huge numbers of British-made vehicles overseas to earn urgently needed foreign currency. This was at the expense of manufacturers investing for the future and designing new models, all of which deprived

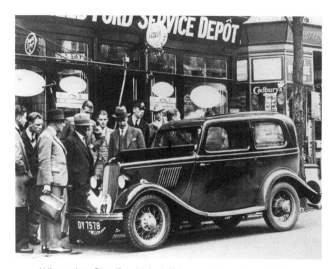

When this 8hp Ford Model Y was pictured outside a Ford Service Depot there was little talk of war. Halcyon days, perhaps, but Britain's military strength was being undermined whilst Germany, under the dictatorship of Adolf Hitler, was amassing its weaponry. It was the mid-1930s when the British Government began making contingency plans to boost its arsenal, a role that the British motor industry, aided by Ford and other manufacturers, helped fulfil. (Author's collection)

motorists at home of new cars. There were plans to nationalise Britain's motor industry, a scheme that, had it materialised, would have extended to oil and petrol supplies, thus giving rise to the government being viewed as adopting anti-motoring policies.

The scarcity of suitable vehicles led to a black market. New cars were immediately changing hands at extortionate prices, and pre-war models were commanding values that were considerably greater than their price when new. For the fortunate few who were able to acquire and afford vehicles there remained the

Austerity Motoring from Armistice until the mid-Fifties

This evocative image also depicts an era before Britain was plunged into war in 1939. The location of Derry & Co's Ford agency remains something of a mystery but it is the very essence of the country garage. Standing alongside the 8hp Model Y is a British-built (Slough) Citroën Traction Avant, a car that was then considered as being radical with its front-wheel drive, chassisless construction, torsion bar suspension and hydraulic braking. (Author's collection)

problem of fuel rationing, which was not withdrawn until May 1950. And just as recovery was in sight, the Suez Crisis erupted, plunging the country into economic depression once more.

The journey through the age of austerity accounts for a period of adversity which generated a feeling of camaraderie, enterprise and innovation.

This Morris is negotiating flooded Main Street at Cockermouth in Cumbria when Britain was desperately building for the war effort, and plans for petrol rationing were being drawn up. (Elaine Williamson)

In Time of War

When war was declared on 3rd September 1939, Britain's motor industry reacted instantly to a dramatic change of direction in order to produce for the war effort. For some of those manufacturers who diversified to build military components, there was no turning back once hostilities were at an end.

The motor industry's role in wartime had been planned in the mid-1930s when threat of conflict exposed Britain's military arsenal to be gravely depleted. In preparation for combat, the Air Ministry devised a scheme whereby motor manufacturers would aid the aircraft industry by building aero engines and associated components to ensure the armed services were equipped.

The arrangement led to the construction of several 'shadow factories' around the country. Sir Hugh Dowding, Head of Supply and Research at the Air Ministry, negotiated with Roy Fedden, who was the Bristol Aircraft Company's chief engineer, to assist in establishing a group of factories in the Midlands to produce Bristol aero engines. Austin, Daimler, Rootes,

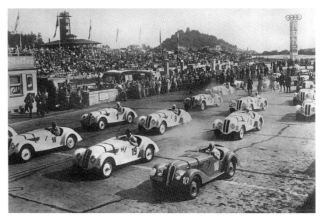

This was the scene at the start in the 2-litre sports car class for a special race held in 1938 at the Nürburgring on the occasion of the German Grand Prix. BMW 328s dominate, and Paul Greifzu, driving car 10, won the event. The winner of the Grand Prix on the 24th July was the British driver Richard Seaman, his success in Germany being received with mixed sentiments, especially when he was wreathed in laurels adorned with the swastika. A little over a year later Britain and Germany were at war. (BMW)

Shadow factories were prime targets for the Luftwaffe and therefore were carefully camouflaged. This is the Rolls-Royce works at Crewe where the walls of the workshops were made to resemble houses. The camouflage was so effective that it remained visible in the 1970s. (Rolls-Royce)

Rover, Singer and Standard were initially enlisted to supplement the dozen or more airframe manufacturers and the four major aero engine suppliers, Armstrong Siddeley, Bristol, Napier and Rolls-Royce. Lord Austin, who chaired the shadow factory scheme, extended it to include a new Rolls-Royce factory at Crewe and a Ford plant at Urmston near Manchester to build Merlin and Griffon engines.

Shadow factories were owned and financed by the government and managed by the motor industry. The Treasury financed the construction of the factories and additionally supported management fees of up to £50,000 per annum, as well as paying £225 per aircraft supplied and £75 for each engine delivered. At the end of the war shadow factories were assigned to the motor industry for motor vehicle production.

While some manufacturers were engaged to build armaments, others continued producing vehicles for the war effort. Both Austin and Ford turned out staff cars, ambulances and troop carriers by the thousand. Elsewhere in the industry, firms such as Hillman, Morris and Standard added to the arsenal of military vehicles while others, like Renault at Acton, provided essential components for tanks. In nearby Slough, Citroën assembled in excess of 23,000 Canadian Military Pattern trucks.

Car production did not cease immediately at the onset of war. During the early weeks of 1940 new car registrations were averaging 3500 per month and Ford bravely introduced the Anglia, of which a little more than 5000 were produced before production ceased. It was not until July that all unregistered cars were seized and purchases of new vehicles banned except for special use, for which a licence was necessary.

There may have been cars at the outbreak of war, but it was a different situation regarding petrol. A month before war was declared a petrol rationing scheme had been devised and this came into effect at the end of September. This allowed for a basic ration calculated on a car's horsepower rating, potentially affording between one and two hundred miles of motoring a month. The allowance was four gallons a month for cars of up to 7hp rating, five gallons for 9hp cars,

Production of marine engines replaced motor vehicles at Renault's works at Acton in West London. In car factories around the country assembly lines were transformed to cater for the war effort, although motor manufacturing did not entirely stop. Commercial and utility vehicles were required in large numbers by the fighting services and firms building them included Austin, Hillman, Humber, Morris and Standard. (Author's collection)

rising to ten gallons for 20hp and above, and for business and essential car users there were supplementary rations.

Petrol companies pooled their resources to make fuel available, thus the introduction of 'pool' petrol. It was considered expensive at a cost commensurate with 10p per gallon, but was substantially cheaper than black market fuel at 35p per gallon. To prevent commercial fuel from being fraudulently sold by profiteers it was dyed red, and anyone caught using it illegally was liable to prosecution. Proving the case was not always easy as the dye could be removed by filtering petrol through gauze. There were more legitimate means of obtaining

Their Majesties King George VI and Queen Elizabeth did much to support and encourage war effort production and here the royal couple can be seen arriving at Crewe to witness the building of Merlin aero engines. The King and Queen's interest in the work that was being conducted at shadow factories around the country was much appreciated and helped boost morale among the nation. (Rolls-Royce)

petrol, such as agreeing to provide transport to service personnel or by making one's car available for lifts. This was known as the 'help your neighbour' scheme, and was sponsored by the government to provide transport for City workers to and from the London suburbs.

Car use during the first six months or so of the war did not diminish quite as quickly as some politicians had expected, and questions were raised in parliament regarding the number of vehicles in use at seaside resorts and sporting events around the country. Car usage was at the mercy of blackout regulations which called for all roadside equipment such as traffic lights, lamp posts, Belisha beacons and bollards to be painted white so that they were more visible at night. Even trees had white swathes painted on them.

Motorists had to paint bumpers and running board sides white and modify headlamps so that one was masked and the bulb removed from the other. Problems occurred when regulations failed to dictate which headlamp should be masked and which bulb should be removed. Sidelights and rear lamps had to be dimmed, the most effective means of doing this was to apply two layers of newspaper to them to diffuse luminance. Accident rates involving motorists and pedestrians were horrific during blackout hours and ultimately parliament introduced a blanket speed limit of 20mph during darkness in built up areas.

In the summer of 1940 when the risk of invasion heightened, all road signs were removed and roads around the southern and eastern coasts of the country were designated restricted areas. Road blocks were set up and anyone not stopping at a check point risked being shot. Drivers were required to immobilise their cars when parking by removing the distributor rotor arm or crossing or disconnecting high tension leads.

Countless private cars were put to use assisting

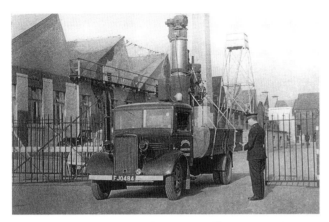

Following the outbreak of war every effort was made to supply equipment for the armed forces. A smart new-looking Morris Commercial lorry is seen at the Morris factory loaded with machinery, its headlamps are masked to comply with blackout regulations. (Author's collection)

with the war effort, but for many owners rationing and blackout regulations made driving impossible and they therefore laid up their vehicles or disposed of them. Some owners of all-steel saloons adopted radical measures by burying their cars in their gardens, utilising them as makeshift air raid shelters. In July 1942 petrol rationing was tightened which meant that supplies were withdrawn from all but essential users, and even tyres were only available to those with special dispensation.

With petrol strictly limited, experiments were carried out using alternative fuels. Motorists could acquire low pressure gas from gasworks, this being stored in a bag on top of a car or in a trailer. Alternatively, gas producers could be used; they burned coal, coke or wood but the power efficiency was considerably less than petrol. Used by commercial operators, gas producers were often dismissed by private motorists on the grounds that they were too expensive to buy and run.

A variety of vehicles were commandeered for the war effort including London taxicabs, the example depicted here having been assigned to the Auxiliary Fire Service. Note the ladder mounted to the cab's roof, the hoses stored on the luggage platform, and the water pump coupled to the vehicle. These cabs were driven by cabbies who were either too old to be enlisted for military service or who were medically unfit to fight. (Author's collection)

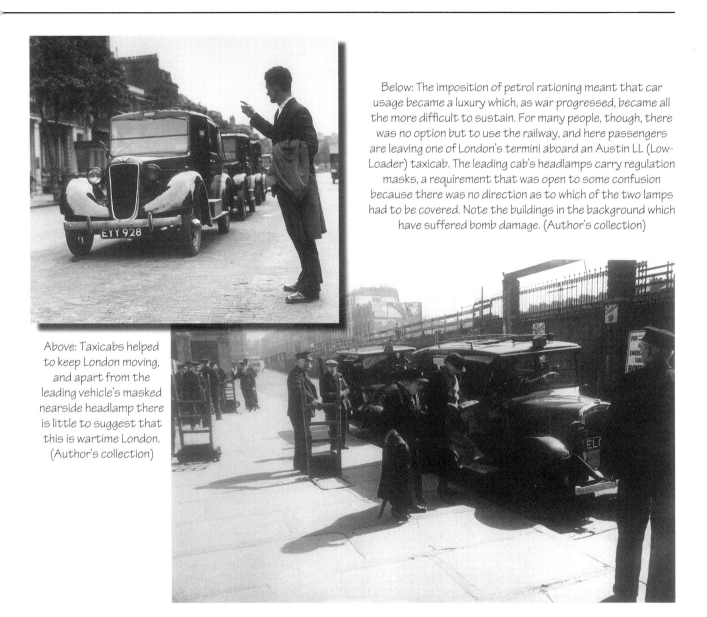

Below: The imposition of petrol rationing meant that car usage became a luxury which, as war progressed, became all the more difficult to sustain. For many people, though, there was no option but to use the railway, and here passengers are leaving one of London's termini aboard an Austin LL (Low-Loader) taxicab. The leading cab's headlamps carry regulation masks, a requirement that was open to some confusion because there was no direction as to which of the two lamps had to be covered. Note the buildings in the background which have suffered bomb damage. (Author's collection)

Above: Taxicabs helped to keep London moving, and apart from the leading vehicle's masked nearside headlamp there is little to suggest that this is wartime London. (Author's collection)

Austerity Motoring from Armistice until the mid-Fifties

Wartime regulations meant that in addition to wearing blackout masks, motor vehicles were required to have bumpers, running boards and wing edges painted white in similar fashion to this Hillman in service with the Metropolitan Police. Local authorities were responsible for painting street furniture white, and roadside trees, which represented particular hazards, were also treated to a coat of whitewash for safety reasons. (Metropolitan Police)

Blackout regulations had been planned some time before the declaration of war and a practice run was ordered for southern and eastern England on the night of 9th/10th August 1939. This Wolseley police car has been suitably prepared, the off-side headlamp having been masked while the bulb in the nearside unit has been removed. In addition to the wing-top sidelamps being masked, white paint has been applied to the wings and running boards. (Metropolitan Police)

The reliability and high efficiency of

MAZDA

CAR
BULBS

Side, Tail
and
Dashlight
Bulb

"U" Filament
Regulation
Headlight
Bulb

are of the greatest
possible assistance in

BLACKOUT DRIVING

Always fit Mazda Headlight
and Sidelight Bulbs

During the war the motoring press carried advertisements
and information aimed at helping motorists cope with
driving under difficult conditions. This Mazda advertisement
appeared in *The Motor* of December 3rd 1941.
(Author's collection)

This Guy Arab omnibus is in service near Wolverhampton.
Bus travel was an essential means of transport, and
services remained in operation throughout difficult
conditions. During the war Guy Motors transferred to
production of military service vehicles.
(Author's collection)

Driving during the blackout was obviously hazardous
for both motorists and pedestrians. The accident rate
during the early period of war increased dramatically, the
deaths on Britain's roads exceeding 8000 for 1939, rising
to 9200 in 1941. This was despite a 20mph speed limit
imposed on all roads during the hours of darkness from
1st February 1940. Commercial vehicles were subject to
the same restrictions as other vehicles, including those
operated by the country's police forces, such as this Black
Maria belonging to the West Yorkshire Constabulary.
(Colin Chipperfield)

Morris Motors at Cowley maximised its efforts producing military vehicles to include Crusader tanks as well as complete aircraft. More mundane government vehicles were also assembled, such as these Morris trucks.
(LAT Photographic)

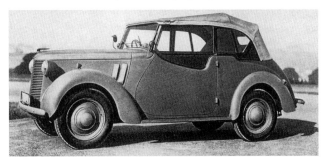

AEC bus production was also frozen in the interests of building military vehicles. Petrol rationing meant that for private motorists car usage was often impossible, and for those with coupons there was always the difficulty of obtaining components with which to keep vehicles running. Bedworth is to the north of Coventry, home of the British motor industry. (Author's collection)

Austin at Longbridge was also contracted to build government vehicles. Among them were six-wheeled four-wheel drive trucks, the legendary K2 Ambulance, Austin 3-ton general service lorries, and the Austin Eight utility vehicle which so successfully undertook liaison and communication duties. In addition, Longbridge built aircraft, marine engines and components for Churchill tanks.
(Author's collection)

Many private cars were utilised for the war effort, including this Morris which lost its coachwork in favour of a utility ambulance body. While car owners voluntarily gave up their cars for war use, thousands of other vehicles were commandeered and converted to ambulances. (Author's collection)

A wide variety of vehicles were put to use in the Second World War. This Rolls-Royce 40/50hp is the property of Moore's of Brighton, motor engineers of Russell Square, for whom it served as a breakdown vehicle and tow truck. This fine motor vehicle has been adopted by the Home Guard which was established to help thwart an enemy invasion. (Sir Henry Royce Memorial Foundation)

In 1940 the Ministry of Home Security considered the prospect of having all private motor vehicles camouflaged. Polished cellulose reflected light and could be easily detected from the air, thus presenting a specific target for enemy aircraft. Original proposals affected only those vehicles operating in or near key defence areas, although commitment remained to extend the scheme if necessary. In some circumstances camouflaging vehicles was essential and the process of applying it is depicted here at R.E.A.L's coachbuilding works of Ealing in West London. The cost of camouflaging a vehicle varied from 35 shillings (£1.17½p) to £5 10s (£5.50p) according to size. (LAT Photographic)

Pictured in London following an air raid in 1940, this Austin, which is the subject of intense discussion by bystanders, suffered severe damage after catching fire. Most common damage was caused to motor vehicles caught by shrapnel and falling masonry, and not least by falling into bomb craters during the blackout. (LAT Photographic)

When petrol rationing was enforced within three weeks of declaration of war on 3rd September 1939, the measure was designed not to eliminate private motoring but to ensure the fair disbursement of supplies to allow adequate fuel for essential users. Alternative fuels were sought by both private motorists and commercial users, the most common being gas, whether it was obtained via the gas mains or a gas producer, a type of which is depicted here and attached to a 12hp Morris. The tall cylinder on the left is the water cooler; next to it is the gas scrubber and filter while the large cylinder is the generator which uses anthracite peas as fuel. The cooler and dust box is on the far right. Seventy pounds of fuel are contained within the generator, which provides some 140 miles of motoring. Running on gas-using producers did not give parity with petrol in respect of performance but it did provide for motoring (averaging 1d per seven miles) should petrol become unavailable. (LAT Photographic)

Austerity Motoring from Armistice until the mid-Fifties

Left: Several types of gas producers were marketed. Here, an experimental producer fitted to the side of a vehicle is being replenished with British coal. (Author's collection)

Above: A more popular method of running on gas was to utilise town gas direct from the mains and store it in a gasbag attached to a car's roof. Supplies of town gas were limited to built-up areas, which precluded ideas of driving deep into the country. Gasbags made vehicles unstable in windy weather, and their continuous flapping and exposure to the elements necessitated frequent repair or replacement.
(LAT Photographic)

SAVE SHIPS—
Convert ESSENTIAL TRANSPORT
to **TOWNS GAS**

WALSH ALL-STEEL EXCELLENT PERFORMANCE
CONVERSION gives LOWER RUNNING COSTS
GAS OR PETROL OPERATION
INSTANT CHANGEOVER
IDENTICAL DRIVING TECHNIQUE

NEIL & MOSTYN LTD.

Telephone:
MACaulay 1252-3

By courtesy "THE AUTOCAR." 262, CLAPHAM ROAD • LONDON • SW 9

Right: While gasbags offered an alternative to petrol, their use was somewhat limited owing to the fact that not everyone had access to gas mains. This contemporary advertisement gives a clue to the extent of the equipment needed to operate on gas. It is estimated that around 1000 private motorists were running their cars fitted with gasbags in 1942. (Author's collection)

Motor manufacturers contributed enormously to the war effort and their dedication is illustrated to good effect in this painting by Helen McKie which adorned the front cover of a publicity book entitled *Ford at War*. The work outlines efforts at Dagenham to produce a wide variety of armaments and vehicles, some of which are depicted here. Ford factories around the world contributed enormously to the war effort. Ford India and Ford Canada built in excess of 134,000 and 395,000 vehicles respectively, while the company's South African plant supplied 34,869 passenger vehicles and delivery wagons. Ford New Zealand produced millions of grenades and bombs in addition to 5200 vehicles of all types. The factory also reconditioned more than a thousand Jeeps that were recovered from the Pacific war zone. (Author's collection)

Export or Die

Before the war was over those motorists who were able to run cars, even as essential users, faced many difficulties. In cities around the country cars were often destroyed as a result of bomb damage or being hit by collapsing buildings. There was the added danger of motorists unwittingly driving into bomb craters at night, owing to poor visibility caused by blackout regulations.

London's taxi fleet was seriously depleted because cabs were requisitioned for civil defence purposes. The cabs' manoeuvrability, courtesy of their tight turning circle, made these vehicles highly desirable for negotiating war-torn streets. London cabbies also played an important role; those too old or unfit for military service were drafted to drive cabs which had been converted to ambulances or pressed into service as auxiliary fire tenders.

The motor industry underwent fundamental change, for before the onset of hostilities it had been a largely male-dominated society. Women were more widely employed and undertook demanding work servicing and repairing army vehicles and staff cars. There was also a rise in the number of unskilled workers drafted in to the industry. Ford, for example, took on substantial numbers of unskilled Irish workers to fulfil foundry jobs, which were among the most unpleasant jobs at Dagenham. The arrangement included two return tickets to Ireland annually, paid for by the Ministry of Labour.

Changes in the industry also came about through negotiations with trade unions, the effects of which determined the government to look at motor manufacturing practice in readiness for peacetime. Not only had the notion of building motorways stemmed from pre-war days, no doubt influenced by Germany's plans for its system of autobahns, but ministers were sure that motor building was regarded as one of the most

The liberation of France and the Armistice that followed summoned thoughts of life returning to some normality. The motor industry in Europe was in tatters, although Britain was well placed for recovery owing to the pre-war establishment of shadow factories which, after hostilities, were assigned mainly to motor manufacturing. Scenes like this epitomise the mood in Europe and serve as a reminder of the importance of the motorcar in society. (Author's collection)

During the war, planning for motor production in peacetime called for some draconian measures, some of which, such as nationalising the motor industry, did not materialise. There had been a call to produce a 'national' car, one that could be mass-produced and was affordable. One person who was well placed to produce this type of vehicle, and was indeed encouraged to do so by government ministers, was Roy Fedden (later Sir Roy) of Bristol aero engine and aircraft fame. Another was William Kendall, MP for Grantham in Lincolnshire, who is seen here with his prototype car in 1945, which he envisaged putting into large scale production at the rate of at least 10,000 vehicles a year. Planning for a people's car went by the wayside, as did proposals to radically change British car building. Neither this nor Fedden's prototype were put into production. (LAT Photographic)

prosperous and successful of Britain's industries.

A document prepared for the government in readiness for reconstructing the motor industry in peacetime was critical about it lacking the potential for mass production. There was concern that the industry could not easily satisfy large scale manufacturing for export, or that there was sufficient will to produce large numbers of high-powered cars. The pre-war production of such cars was courtesy of a relatively few low-volume manufacturers. The course the industry had taken

was for a preference towards lower powered vehicles, of which there were too many models and little or no standardization of components.

The government committee given charge to consider post-war manufacturing pored over several proposals. Not least was a notion to rationalise it, leading to nationalisation. In November 1945, Sir Stafford Cripps addressed the Society of Motor Manufacturers and Traders (SMMT) telling delegates that Britain must provide a tough, decent-sized car of good appearance. His message quite clearly indicated that every effort had to be put into producing for export, and therefore cars that were deemed suitable for the home market and designed for mainly making short journeys over smooth roads would not necessarily suffice abroad. Instead, the industry needed to diversify and mass-produce vehicles in huge quantities, and in order to achieve this only the

When Rover resumed car manufacturing the company envisaged building a quality small saloon much the same size as the Fiat Topolino. The result was the 700cc M1. It was abandoned following the government's call to nationalise the motor industry and a one-make-one-model policy. (Author's collection)

best designs would be acceptable to motorists at home and overseas.

Cripps had been influenced by a number of motor industry personalities drafted into the Ministry of Supply to advise the government on wartime production of vehicles. In early 1943 the SMMT had campaigned to permit manufacturers to plan for post-war production by considering new designs and preparing prototypes. Hopes of an early return to car building were dashed when, later in the year, the SMMT announced that there would be no new models for some time.

There was some resistance to producing completely new models. William Morris, for example, was totally opposed to progressing the design of the Minor, which he disliked, preferring instead to continue with the pre-war Eight. Others, such as Sir Roy Fedden, were keen to promote innovative designs, his own medium-sized saloon with its rear-mounted three-cylinder,

air-cooled radial engine being proposed for large-scale production to satisfy British and European markets. Backing Fedden's scheme, the government found itself at odds with several manufacturers who believed a more conservative approach to future production needed to be considered. As it happened, Fedden's project failed to materialise, mainly because of the proposed car's revolutionary design and limited resources with which to develop it. Ironically, the concept of a mass-produced rear-engined car was rejected by the same British motor industry that discarded the Volkswagen.

It was early 1944 when permission was given to a limited number of firms to undertake experimental and preparatory work in advance of resuming car production. By October the number of licenses issued to manufacturers had risen to 56. The will to take up the challenge of producing a national car, or series of national models, had been lost, and in many instances

With the resumption of car building, the government left manufacturers in no doubt as to the importance of producing vehicles for export. Quantities of steel and other raw materials were in short supply so consideration was given only to those manufacturers who were capable of producing at least 50 percent, the figure later increasing to 75 percent, of their output for export sales. This is the scene at the Nuffield factory at Cowley where a line of Morris Tens are destined for India and other overseas markets. On the right of the picture can be seen a line of Morris Eights in the course of assembly. (Author's collection)

manufacturers merely revamped their pre-war designs.

The motor industry was in conflict with the government regarding motor taxation, an issue that was argued both in parliament and within the pages of the leading motoring journals. The SMMT wanted a flat-rate tax based on cylinder capacity, but instead a graduated scheme was adopted, the tax rising by 100cc steps in accordance with an engine's cubic capacity.

In 1945 the SMMT announced that the industry would potentially produce 200,000 vehicles in 1946. In the early autumn Sir Stafford Cripps called for 30 percent of production to be exported, raising the figure to 50 percent within weeks. The figure was again increased, this time to 75 percent. Arguments regarding taxation returned and Hugh Dalton, Chancellor of the Exchequer, announced that from January 1948 a flat-rate tax of £10 would be applied to all cars first registered after January 1947. In acknowledging that revenue would be lost on the most powerful cars, he announced the doubling of purchase tax from 33 to 66 percent on vehicles costing more than £1000.

In 1948 the export drive was shown to be of such importance that George Strauss, the Minister of Supply, announced that steel supplies would only be made available to those manufacturers exporting 75 percent of their output. In a chilling message to the motor industry, he made it abundantly clear that he was willing to see firms go out of business if they were unable to achieve such targets.

The industry boomed as export targets were met and exceeded, the demand for cars worldwide being satisfied by a proliferation of small to medium-sized British saloons. The industry's success was such that in 1950 Britain was the world's biggest exporter of cars. The target to build 200,000 cars in 1946 was exceeded by 19,000, and a million cars were being built annually by 1958. By 1954 British exports were levelling off while those of France and Germany were soaring. Britain, however, was a victim of the Suez Crisis in 1956 and the country's lead in the export stakes was overtaken by West Germany ...

The first post-war British cars to be exported to the Middle East were these Standards which were disembarked at Haifa in December 1945. On the far left is a Standard Tourer which is accompanied by three 8hp models. On the far right is the larger 12/14hp. The cars are awaiting collection from the port by Palestine Motors, the sole Standard agent in Palestine and Transjordan. (LAT Photographic)

Morris Minors and Rileys being prepared for export at Cowley. Not all cars destined for export were crated in this manner, others were taken to ports aboard car transporters and loaded onto ships. The Morris Minor owes its development to Alec Issigonis, one of the most respected designers and engineers, who first considered ideas to replace the Morris Eight in pre-war days and who produced the Mosquito prototype, which eventually emerged as the Minor. (Author's collection)

Longbridge was also heavily involved in producing for export. This picture dates from July 1945 and shows Austin Ten four-door saloons undergoing final inspection on the assembly lines shortly after the production lines were reinstated. On the adjacent production line K2 ambulances are being prepared, these vehicles having performed an essential service during wartime. In total some 13,000 K2s were built at Longbridge. (Author's collection/*Autocar*)

Flying the flag for Britain, the Nuffield Organisation exported its products to the USA. This evocative advertisement depicts a Morris Minor and MG vying with traffic in New York. The marketing message was simple and effective: British products satisfied American customers in respect of build quality, running costs and the ease with which such cars as the Minor and MG Sports could be manoeuvred along crowded streets and into parking-places. The image of Americans choosing British cars was obviously a fillip at a time it was most needed, and such sales brought much needed foreign currency. (Author's collection)

WE'RE PART OF THE AMERICAN SCENE, TOO!

You might think that a country with 39 million cars and a production of 6,680,000 more every year would be able to supply all its needs. But the fact remains that since the war Nuffield products have become extremely popular in the U.S. And each has brought home much-needed hard currency to help Britain's vital balance of trade.

The reason for our success is simple. The U.S. does not produce anything in their class quite so good as, or quite like, those two Nuffield favourites, the Morris Minor and the M.G. Sports, which have formed the bulk of Nuffield's car exports to the Americas.

The American motorist, with the constant (and increasing) problem of crowded traffic and overcrowded parking-places, has been quick to see the advantage of these small and manoeuvrable quality-cars. He gives full marks to their quick getaway from the lights and their ability to "park on a dime". And he doesn't exactly object to their running-economy either. Despite the rising cost of petrol, he doesn't have to dig so deeply into his pocket.

Before 1945, it was unusual to see a British car on the American roads. Nowadays, when one of these Nuffield thoroughbreds slips out of the car-park and across the green lights, it seems to have become an established part of the kaleidoscopic American scene.

NUFFIELD ORGANIZATION

MORRIS · WOLSELEY · RILEY · M.G. · MORRIS-COMMERCIAL
NUFFIELD TRACTORS · MORRIS MARINE & INDUSTRIAL ENGINES

NUFFIELD PRODUCTS

Overseas Business : Nuffield Exports Limited, Cowley, Oxford, and at 41 Piccadilly, London, W.1

Between 1948 and 1950 in excess of 78,000 Morris Minors were built, a high percentage of them being exported to markets around the world including Australia, New Zealand, the USA, India and Europe. Morris advertising proclaimed the Minor to be 'The World's Supreme Small Car', and this cannot be far from the truth judging by the numbers that have survived. LHD Minors are seen here being driven aboard transporters in readiness for despatch to port. (Author's collection)

Trade drivers employed by The Car Collection Company delivered Hillmans and Humbers from the Rootes Group factory at Ryton-on-Dunsmore to London, from where they were shipped abroad. Much care was taken en-route from Coventry to the Thames, with convoys of cars halting at regular intervals to enable drivers to check oil and water levels. Car Collection Company drivers were all a minimum of 33 years old with ten or more years' driving experience: a British School of Motoring test was obligatory (with a pass mark of not below 85 percent). (Author's collection/*The Motor*)

Dagenham's motor production resumed at the end of May 1945, just three weeks after VE Day. The first post-war production car to leave the factory was an 8hp Anglia on 21st June, a machine which, like its stablemate the Prefect, was a revived pre-war model. All haste was made to re-equip the factory when car production resumed; chassis assemblies are shown being constructed in this picture. (Ford)

Ford's contribution to the export drive was in line with other manufacturers, with vehicles being transported to a wide overseas market. The 8hp Anglia was in production at the Essex Thames-side works until 1948, after which a new model - which was surprisingly similar to that in pre-war production - was introduced to become the cheapest car on the UK market (not including three-wheelers). Economy went further than mere price, and contemporary motoring journals were critical about its road-holding behaviour and handling characteristics. For all that though, the car was well received by motorists. (Ford)

FORD CARS 1938-49

PREFECT 10 HP 1938

ANGLIA 8 HP 1939

ANGLIA 8 HP 1946

V8 PILOT 30 HP 1947

ANGLIA 8 HP 1949

PREFECT 10 HP 1949

After the gap of a decade, the London Motor Show resumed in the autumn of 1948 and had a record number of visitors. 'If Britain cannot buy cars at least it likes to see them', was reported in *Autocar*. Earls Court captured the post-war atmosphere of expectation, even if the political climate was anything but hopeful. This is Ford's display showing the Anglia in good company with the V8 Pilot and, partially hidden, the Prefect. In times of austerity the Pilot was a bold move, but a contentious one within the Ford boardroom. The car was very much an eleventh hour job, the original design having been discarded. The new model sported an all-new 2½ litre V8 engine, which failed to provide the anticipated performance, and the 30hp V8, which was already in production, was fitted instead. (Ford)

The Ford catalogue for the period 1938 to 1949 shows the models' family resemblance, all of which were bought by car-starved motorists at home and abroad. (Ford)

Engineering expertise! This is the view within the confines of the Bristol Aeroplane Company. In 1948, the huge eight-engined Brabazon 224-seater airliner was being built for transatlantic service. The car is the Bristol 400 2 litre coupé which was first announced in 1945 with deliveries commencing in 1947. Few Bristol motorcars were built for the home market, the majority of vehicles were exported. Bristol motorcars were based on the BMW chassis and built by the Car and Light Engineering Division of the aircraft company, the Chairman being George White, while Major George Abell, who had previously worked for Invicta, was General Manager. (LAT Photographic)

Two generations of small Fords are pictured here, a 103E Popular ahead of a 100E Prefect. Both cars were in production from 1953 until 1959, although derivatives of the latter lived on until 1962. The Popular was, in effect, a re-worked export edition Anglia, having the most basic of specification to include a painted metal instrument board, a single windscreen wiper and plastic-faced floor felt. (Ford)

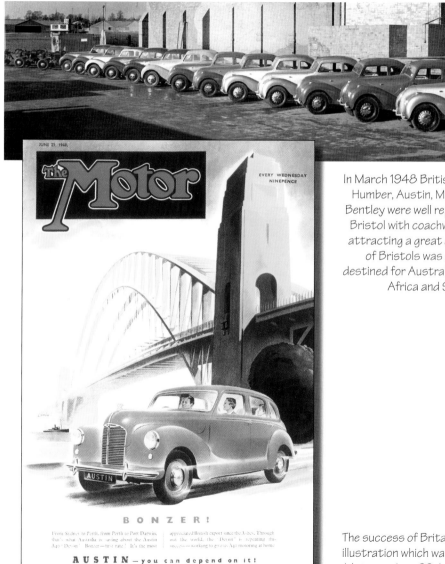

In March 1948 British cars such as Rover, Standard, Hillman, Humber, Austin, Morris, Riley, Jaguar and Rolls-Royce and Bentley were well represented at the Geneva Motor Show. A Bristol with coachwork by Touring of Milan was also shown, attracting a great deal of attention. Meanwhile a shipment of Bristols was awaiting despatch from the factory, destined for Australia, Belgium, Brazil, Czechoslovakia, South Africa and Switzerland. (LAT Photographic)

The success of Britain's export drive is exemplified by this illustration which was carried on the front cover of *The Motor* on June 29th 1948. (Author's collection/ *The Motor*)

Keeping Going

The Armistice summoned hope and prosperity, and if motorists were encouraged by news that a resumption of motor production signalled a return to some normality, their aspirations were short-lived.

Petrol rationing remained in force until May 1950, during which time motorists sought the utmost economy, even invoking innovative means to eke out fuel or using petrol substitutes. The absence of new cars meant that there was a market for ex-War Department vehicles that were suitably converted for domestic and commercial use. Following war usage such vehicles were dumped in compounds around the country, and motor dealers, recognising there to be a ready and lucrative market, keenly negotiated terms with the appropriate ministry.

It was common for dealers to rescue those vehicles that could be easily and quickly re-commissioned. They renovated engines and transmissions, removed existing bodies and fitted utilitarian coachwork.

Some of the specialists offering utility bodies for ex-War Department vehicles became synonymous with the post-war coachbuilding industry. Operating from Melton Court in South Kensington, Harold Radford & Co. advertised a varied selection of guaranteed reconditioned cars along with a variety of commercial vehicles. In the years that followed, Harold Radford became renowned for its Countryman conversions on a selection of designs that included Humbers, Armstrong Siddeleys, Jaguars, Rolls-Royces and Bentleys.

Another utility specialist was Martin Walter Ltd. of Folkestone, which produced pre-war coachwork for some of the most prestigious motorcars. Utilecon conversions led the firm to become synonymous with Dormobile motor caravans which emerged in 1954 and remained in vogue for some forty years.

One of the best known and most familiar of post-war vehicles was born when Maurice Wilks bought an army surplus Jeep, thus sowing an idea which germinated into the Land Rover.

For car owners putting their vehicle back on the road after it was laid up for such a long time, there was much advice in the motoring press. The need for careful re-commissioning was obvious, and all journals of the period carried step-by-step instructions. Sales of pre-war cars were widely advertised and, because of the absence of new models, commanded much inflated values, many exceeding their price when new.

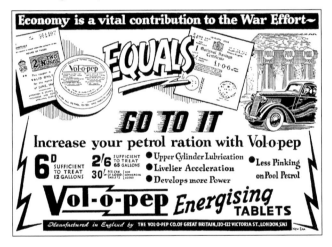

A number of products and fuel additives were advertised which claimed to improve a vehicle's fuel consumption. 6d worth (2½p) of Vol-o-pep energising tablets was sufficient to treat 12 gallons of pool petrol. How many motorists actually used such products is not known, but advertisements frequently appeared in the motoring press for the duration of petrol rationing. After 1942 petrol rationing became all the more acute when basic rations were withdrawn and supplies reserved for essential users. (Author's collection)

A number of commodities appeared on the market aimed at increasing a car's economy. In addition to carburettor manufacturers reassuring customers that their merchandise offered the most economical motoring, it was possible to purchase fuel additives in order to make the most of meagre petrol rations. Vol-o-pep energising tablets was one such product, with 6d (2½p) being sufficient to treat 12 gallons of pool petrol. The supplier's claim was that the tablets provided upper cylinder lubrication, afforded livelier acceleration, developed more power and, to some extent, eliminated pinking.

Grundy's Petroids were also popular, the claim being they gave 20 percent greater fuel economy. Redex oil additive was also widely available, the customary red can a familiar sight at garage forecourts well into the 1960s. According to advertisements placed in the popular press, the Plus-Gas generator, using special crystals, afforded 61mpg fuel economy at 30mph on an 8hp car. The price for such economy was 45 shillings, with replacement crystal refills costing 5 shillings to provide for around 2500 miles of motoring.

Shortages of raw materials was an on-going problem, especially rubber for tyres. 'Ransack your home for rubber' was the message carried in all newspapers during the war, such was the urgent national need to salvage waste rubber of every kind. The deficiency in supplies from the Far East was causing concern to the military forces, hence the call to garner rubber products for recycling. Old rubber tyres, whether from motorcars, prams or bicycles, were as essential as garden hoses, hot water bottles and wringer rollers. Introduction of draconian measures meant that it became impossible to sell tyres unless they came complete with a car!

Tyre manufacturers encouraged worn tyres to be returned to their factories for retreading, an often

Supplies of rubber virtually ceased following the fall of Singapore and Malaya in February 1942. Sales of tyres were banned unless sold with the car to which they were fitted, and essential users could only acquire new ones at the discretion of divisional petroleum officers. Notices were placed in all newspapers and motoring journals asking the population to be vigilant and salvage all rubber household commodities. (Author's collection)

criticised process because of inferior practices undertaken by a number of rogue traders. Tyresoles of Wembley was at the forefront of the retreading process. It carried out a reliable service removing worn treads and replacing them with a new surface. This was stitched on and cured at the same time as the new tread was applied (around ½in. thickness).

Synthetic tyres, which were developed in the 1930s and delivered from the spring of 1940, proved to be all the more durable than those made from natural rubber and, whilst more expensive to make, were soon appreciated as being cost-effective.

To get extended use from worn-out and punctured tyres, motorists resorted to stuffing them with hay in order to maintain traction. Another practice was to place oversized covers on top of worn tyres, even if it meant that they fitted clumsily to the wheel rim and restricted driving speeds.

Even after the war the same urgency to economise remained. Remoulds and retreads were popular because they were less expensive than new tyres. The Ministry of Supply took out advertisements in newspapers reminding drivers to take care of tyres by avoiding overloading, adhering to speed limits and checking pressures weekly.

For those motorists keen that their cars should not display the effects of being laid up, a selection of products promised to transform a vehicle's condition to make it look as new. A few coats of Corroid jet black enamel applied to wings, chassis, wheels and other metal parts was all that was required to see worn surfaces and rust magically disappear. A couple of applications of Valay interior cleaner helped renovate seats, roofcloth and carpets, but if leather upholstery had completely deteriorated there was always Rexine or Duranide with which to replace it.

Salvaging worn rubber tyres meant that they could be processed for further use. Tyresoles of Wembley was among a number of specialists that recycled tyres by retreading them. The process involved removing all trace of the worn tread and applying a new surface, onto which a tread pattern was formed. Retreading tyres in this manner continued throughout the years of austerity and well into the 1960s. (Author's collection)

Good times are just around the corner - or were they? When this emotive illustration graced the cover of *The Autocar* on 2nd March 1945 plans were already being made to resume car production at factories around Britain. This Series III Wolseley summoned the revival of pre-war designs that heralded post-war production. (Author's collection)

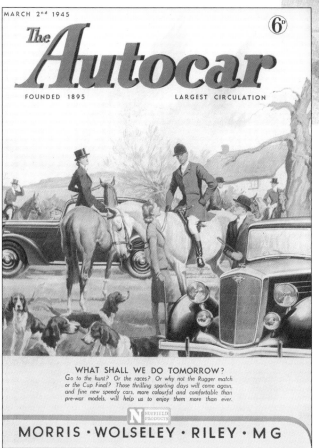

MARCH 2ⁿᵈ 1945

The **Autocar**

FOUNDED 1895   LARGEST CIRCULATION

6ᴅ

WHAT SHALL WE DO TOMORROW?
Go to the hunt? Or the races? Or why not the Rugger match or the Cup Final? Those thrilling sporting days will come again, and fine new speedy cars, more colourful and comfortable than pre-war models, will help us to enjoy them more than ever.

N NUFFIELD PRODUCTS

MORRIS · WOLSELEY · RILEY · MG

Motorists unable to afford, let alone acquire, post-war models were satisfied with pre-war models that commanded inflated prices due to demand. In this London street two eclectic designs are evident, a Fiat 500A Topolino which was registered only a month before declaration of war, and a RHD British-assembled Citroën Traction Avant which carries wedding ribbons. The Fiat was among the smallest cars on the market while the Citroën was a firm favourite with those connected with motor sport. (Author's collection)

Getting a car into a presentable condition was one thing, but obtaining components to keep it running was another. Pistons, water pumps, clutch plates and carburettors were simply unavailable unless one had access to a manufacturing source or was prepared to buy on the black market.

During the years immediately following the Armistice it was not unusual to see cars fitted with odd headlamps or displaying strange modifications merely in order to keep them running. In time such innovation ended with the introduction of the Ministry of Transport Test.

Unable to afford anything like a new car, these Rolls-Royce apprentices, pictured in the mid-1950s, were content to run around in a 1936 Austin Seven, which they fondly referred to as The Heap. (Martin Bourne)

Motorists fortunate enough to own a car at the end of the war were at the mercy of petrol rationing and even the most basic essentials to keep their cars running. This Tecalemit advertisement evoked memories of better times, and hopes for a more profitable future. Advertisements such as the one depicted here served as a useful means of maintaining morale during what was a very difficult era. Blissful domestic scenes, such as the one implied, centred on the family unit; even the pet dog added to the overall feeling of comfort and security. (Author's collection)

FREEDOM!

The same happy preparations for the run; the same keen anticipation of the joys of the open road, so long denied . . . and, incidentally, thanks to Tecalemit Service, the same old car—in fine fettle despite years of enforced inactivity.

When the joys of motoring return make ready for the King's Highway. Tecalemit Maintenance Service will again ensure care-free motoring at its best, so in due course see that your new car has a fair start in life.

TECALEMIT

TECALEMIT LIMITED   GREAT WEST ROAD, BRENTFORD, MIDDX.   Phone: EALing 6661 (16 lines)   HYDRAULIC & MECHANICAL, DESIGNING & MANUFACTURING ENGINEERS

GIRLING LIMITED, GARRISON LANE, BIRMINGHAM, 9

Left: Girling was another manufacturer who could be accused of publishing propaganda; the grim war time scene giving way to times more prosperous. The suggestion of the happy use of motorcars in 1945, without petrol rationing and car ownership restrictions, must have come as a bleak reminder to readers of the motoring press. (Author's collection)

Right: A number of component and material manufacturers dwelled on the prospect of better times, just as this October 1945 Bury Felt advertisement does. (Author's collection)

With the great majority of car production destined for export, the demand for any type of motorcar in the immediate post-war years created a black market with pre-war vehicles commanding hugely inflated prices. For motorists in need of a car, there was always the option of sourcing one of the many vehicles that had been used on military service which were collected in compounds around the country. There was a healthy market for such machines which underwent conversion and renovation before being sold on. (LAT Photographic)

Many cars, like this Vauxhall, were laid up during the war. Supported on blocks to prevent wheel and tyre distortion while the car was stationary, it was now time to re-commission it. Thick dust on the car's exterior is evident, but all the more curious is the vehicle's owner, who is undertaking a messy job whilst dressed in a suit. (LAT Photographic)

Having re-commissioned their cars many motorists would have been tempted to give them a coat of enamel paint to restore the metal to a bright finish. How effective this was can only be imagined. (Author's collection)

The re-commissioning process of a car could extend to the fitting of a car radio, which in 1945 was a luxury item. (Author's collection)

Restoration of basic petrol rationing in 1945 allowed motorists to take to the roads again, and the first organised rally was the M.C.C. event held at Wrotham Park, Barnet in mid-June. More than 60 cars and 250 people attended in glorious sunshine, summoning many to picnic on the lawns. According to the news item in the motoring press, not everyone arrived by car as some made the journey by train. (LAT Photographic)

One person who did take his car to Wrotham Park was racing driver Mike Couper. His car, still with its nearside headlamp masked, is a Slough-built Citroën Big Fifteen roadster, one of five known to have been built in 1940. Mike Couper, who owned a Rolls-Royce and Bentley agency at St. Albans in Hertfordshire, bought the car when he visited Citroën's factory. His attire is typical of the period, and it was customary for him to participate in the Monte dressed in a suit. The car, incidentally, is the sole survivor of its type. (LAT Photographic)

The work of the Jeep during hostilities influenced development of the Land Rover in 1947. Maurice Wilks of the Rover Company decided that this was the type of vehicle that the firm should build, and he was right, for the Land Rover became one of the most familiar and revered motor vehicles of the post-war era. This fine advertisement appeared in the pages of *Country Life* to appeal to a select clientele. (Author's collection)

Traffic on the Brighton Road at Horley in Surrey was heavy on the August Bank Holiday in 1945. On a warm and sunny day motorists are heading to the coast in the knowledge that war is over. There is an interesting mix of vehicles, the leading car being a Standard, followed by a Morris and an Austin. Behind the two coaches is an Austin K2 ambulance. Note the masked headlamps, relics of the blackout. (LAT Photographic)

Among the first vehicles to go into production after the war was the Wolseley Oxford taxicab. Designed pre-war, a prototype amassed a sizeable mileage before the resumption of car production. Parked on Westminster Bridge, these cabs are waiting to move across the Thames on the day of the Royal Wedding on 20th November 1947. (Author's collection)

When Austin launched the FX3 taxicab in 1948 it became London's 'black cab' and was eventually adopted for use in many provincial cities. This contrived publicity photograph successfully depicts the fashions of the late 1940s and early '50s, and the absence of other traffic and parked vehicles is in keeping with the austerity of the time. (Author's collection)

St Giles Circus as seen in the early 1950s. The Dominion Theatre, on the right, is presenting 'Battle of Powder River' while Horne Brothers Limited, a respected clothing emporium, is having a sale. Notable is the almost complete absence of private cars, the traffic mainly comprising buses and taxicabs. (Hulton Getty Picture Library)

Road safety training was given to school children after the war. This mock road accident serves to provide a graphic lesson courtesy of the Metropolitan Police. A cyclist, having been knocked from his bicycle by the driver of the Hillman, is receiving first aid while police take all the necessary particulars and direct traffic. The Wolseley police car is typical of that used by the Metropolitan Police and other forces in the late 1940s and early '50s. (Metropolitan Police)

A sunny bank holiday has encouraged motorists to venture out, but an unfortunate driver has been stopped by police on a busy three lane road. By immediate post-war standards the traffic flow is heavy. Petrol rationing meant that motorists could expect to achieve around 250 miles a month and therefore cars were used mainly for essential journeys as well as the occasional pleasure trip. (Metropolitan Police)

A familiar sight at docks and railway stations around the country was the Scammell Scarab mechanical horse. Depicted in Manchester around 1949, these three-wheeled tractor units were highly manoeuvrable, a requirement when working at ports and on railway station platforms. (Author's collection)

For many people in the period of austerity, car ownership was never affordable, which meant that coach travel was popular. The vagaries of travelling by coach meant that vehicles sometimes broke down, as happened on this occasion in 1953 whilst a Grey-Green was en-route from Torquay to London. Pushing a coach called for a lot of effort, as well as providing some light relief, as can be seen from the faces of the passengers, both aboard the vehicle and those doing all the hard work. (Author's collection)

A New Car?

In 1946 the pages of *The Autocar* and *The Motor* were filled with tempting reports of new cars that were being rushed into production by manufacturers who had little time to prepare new designs. Some of the new cars were, therefore, not so new in concept, but that

did not matter to those motorists who were at the end of lengthy waiting lists. As if to reflect the depressed state of the motor industry, all hopes of resurrecting the London Motor Show in October were dashed when the SMMT decided to postpone Britain's motoring showcase until 1948.

The frustration that motorists endured seeing sleek new designs in the knowledge that they were not available can only be imagined. The 1½ litre Riley Twelve was just one example; a true thoroughbred epitomising all that was special about British sports saloons. All the more enticing was news about the eminent motor sport competitor Donald Healey who was developing a 2.4 litre sportscar.

Not so new was the Wolseley Ten which *The Autocar* described as being 'debonair' in character. First seen in 1939 as the Morris Ten, it featured a separate chassis in place of unitary construction, which in many respects was a retrograde step, but one that nevertheless gave the marque a particular credence. The Morris connection was furthered with the introduction of the Wolseley Eight, an up-market version of the pre-war Morris Eight. The epitome of refinement was the Lanchester, which the motoring press dubbed 'A Modern Quality Ten'. The usual touches of sophistication were evident, such as leather upholstery, even if they did appear somewhat austere.

Following Herbert Austin's death in 1941 his motoring empire was under the command of Leonard Lord. Car production resumed at Longbridge in the

In the first week of 1945 *The Motor* carried this evocative advertisement on its cover. It certainly is an idyllic scene, and one that summoned enthusiasm for buying a new car, depending on affordability and the numbers of vehicles available for the home market. (Author's collection)

summer of 1945 with the 8, 10, 12 and 16hp models, all having pre-war origins, and it was not until 1947 that new designs emerged, mostly for export. Keen

developments were in progress at Longbridge: the A30 with its chassisless construction was seen as the all-new Austin Seven, while the superbly attractive and stylish

This catalogue rendering by Frank Wootton depicting the Armstrong Siddeley Lancaster is highly evocative for it reflects the quest to apply advancing aero technology to cars. (Author's collection)

A90 Atlantic was aimed at American customers and was jealously regarded by hopeful British motorists. Meanwhile at Cowley, Morris was having initial

WOLSELEY

The Trustworthy Car

A NUFFIELD PRODUCT

By the first weeks of 1945 a number of car manufacturers were enticing would-be customers to buy new cars. This Wolseley retains its headlamp masking, a gentle reminder of war. (Author's collection)

difficulties with its delightful little Minor in respect of boardroom quarrels regarding design and engine configuration. Alec Issigonis' ultimate offering is the car that everyone, apart from Lord Nuffield, of course, loved.

A 10hp Prefect was the millionth Ford to leave the Thames-side factory in August 1946. In essence the model was identical to its pre-war ancestor, the 1939 E93A, save for some discreet styling changes. A new Prefect was announced in time for the 1948 London Motor Show, although it was new only in its dressed state as the running gear remained as before. Ford's first 'all-new' post-war model was the Pilot which was introduced in 1947. Sharing the bodyshell with the pre-war V8, but subtly modernised with a new bonnet and radiator grille, the Pilot's new 2½ litre engine was supplanted with the proven 3.6 litre V8 in order to improve performance. The Pilot was hardly austerity conscious and was favoured by a select professional clientele for whom acquisition of extra petrol coupons was not a problem.

In 1947 Luton began offering Vauxhall drivers pre-war designs that were hardly updated. 1948 Wyvern and Velox models continued such ancestry, albeit with slightly smoother exteriors, and it was not until 1951 that the Chevrolet-inspired designs appeared with their glitzy interiors.

Rootes also relied on pre-war designs to spearhead post-war production in 1945. In 1947 the Phase II Hillman Minx replaced the Phase I, which owed its origins to 1939, and was in production for a year when an all-new Minx, the Phase III, made its debut. If the new Minx resembled styling that emanated from America it was because Raymond Loewy, hired by Rootes to advise on design matters, based his ideas on the Studebaker, just as he did for Rover. Humber models also demonstrated American ideas, while Singer was perceived to be the upmarket Hillman. Sunbeam and Sunbeam-Talbot gave little to austerity with their sporting images, the cars being as much at home competing in the gruelling Monte Carlo Rally as they were on leafy roads.

There was innovation, however, and none more so than the Gerald Palmer-designed Jowett Javelin with its boxer engine and streamlined styling. Camouflaging its 1934 origins exceptionally well was Citroën's front-wheel

MORRIS
– My Car

Never failed me, my old Morris, peace *or* war . . . what a gruelling she's had. And when a new car takes her place you bet I'll say 'Morris' again.

N A NUFFIELD PRODUCT

MORRIS   MOTORS   LTD.,   COWLEY,   OXFORD

These two advertisements for Morris Motors Ltd are seven months apart and depict a progressive marketing message. The earlier of the two uses a wartime theme and is masculine in nature; the latter is aimed at the family unit and incorporates the reassurance of a quiet village scene. (Author's collection)

NEW *features in the*

MORRIS "TEN"

This most popular car is now becoming available against M.O.W.T. Licence.

Remember all the advantages of the pre-war MORRIS. Now it's even better. There's more rigid construction, road springs interleaved for silence, rubber mounted front and rear shackles, new design front and double acting rear shock absorbers for smoother riding. The body has still greater attention to detail finish; including new style door trimming, highly effective draught-excluding doors closing with carriage-like quietness, improved trunk-lid sealing rubbers, anti-corrosive waterproofed floor, and many other developments in detail for comfort, longer life and efficiency.

That's why *"I'm going to have a Morris"*.

Series M 10 Fixed Head Saloon   £295 0 0
Purchase Tax   82 13 11
" " Sliding Head Saloon   £305 0 0
Purchase Tax   85 9 5
Prices include spare wheel and tyre.

N A NUFFIELD PRODUCT

MORRIS MOTORS LIMITED · COWLEY · OXFORD

Coming soon

VAUXHALL

10 hp ★ 12 hp ★ 14 hp

A range of Vauxhall cars embodying all the engineering features of the immediate pre-war (1940) models, but with many improvements and refinements, will be available against licences to acquire, from November 1945. Prices will be announced later.

May we remind 10 h.p. motorists that the post-war Vauxhall Ten, will, of course, have the roomier body of the "1940" model, which had only just started in production when war broke out.

NOVEMBER
1945

VAUXHALL MOTORS LIMITED
LUTON, BEDS.

Vauxhall, anticipating post-war car production of its pre-war 10, 12 and 14hp models in October 1945, fails to mention what prices can be expected. (Author's collection)

drive and unitary Light Fifteen, which was built at Slough. Renault, too, found favour with more adventurous motorists with the little Acton-built 4CV which was marketed as the 750.

Flying the flag for Britain, customers were drawn to Standard, although the diminutive 8hp and the substantially larger 12/14hp were leftovers from 1939. The Vanguard with its bulbous Plymouth-influenced body was a different matter, however, with its 2 litre engine hardly promising great economy. The new Standard Eight of 1953 was austere, for it demonstrated few creature comforts, insignificant interior trim, sliding windows and no external boot access.

For those unable to afford a 'proper' motorcar there was always the prospect of a motorcycle combination or minicar, the Bond having particular appeal. Reliant's Regal was all the more car-like, as was the slightly more upmarket AC three-wheeler. Real economy arrived with the Messerschmitt and its tandem seating arrangement, while the Gordon, with its single door and engine uncomfortably close to the driver's seat, afforded little luxury. Bubblecars arrived in time for the Suez Crisis, but for those who wanted fuel economy with comfort - but little in the way of interior sophistication - there was always the 2CV. Such was this tin snail's lack of speed, courtesy of a feeble 375cc air-cooled flat-twin engine, there was no requirement for a fuel gauge other than a dip-stick in the petrol tank. For the great majority of car-starved motorists, this nissen hut on wheels was simply too austere.

The British motor industry might well have been experiencing the short-term fruits of success, but, nevertheless, a serious mistake was made and an opportunity lost. When motor industry chiefs evaluated the Volkswagen works in British occupied Germany they refused to accept its product had a future. Henry Ford

also dismissed it, and ultimately VW was returned to the German nation. By deriding the Beetle, Volkswagen was, within half a decade, allowed to become one of the world's largest and most successful car builders, ultimately owning even that bastion of Britishness, Bentley.

As old as the industry - as modern as the hour. Riley's advertising for its superlative 1½ litre model was bound to influence prospective customers, the styling of the car becoming recognised as classic. A good measure of artistic licence has been used here, the lines of the car having been exaggerated to exciting effect. (Author's collection)

Within six months of the appearance of this Austin advertisement, production at Longbridge was under way. Orders flooded in to the sales department, but shortages of raw materials meant that production was a long way below capacity. (Author's collection)

When the British commanding forces took control of the German Volkswagen works, no one in the British motor industry appreciated its value. It was offered to several manufacturers, including Ford, who turned it down. Major Ivan Hirst and Colonel Charles Radclyffe, seen here, were among those that did recognise what it had to offer and successfully re-established Beetle production. (Volkswagen)

The 1000th Volkswagen being driven off the assembly line at Wolfsburg in March 1946 with Major Hirst at the wheel. In austerity the Beetle helped Germany's economy and served to provide thousands of families with essential transport. (Volkswagen)

Islington, London, in 1946. The scene is one of austerity, the light volume of traffic being halted to allow a Humber police car to proceed, obviously on a 999 call. The Fifty Shilling Tailors was a chain of popular men's outfitters where demobbed servicemen could buy their 'civvy' suits for 50 shillings! (Metropolitan Police)

Production of Vauxhalls was under way at Luton when this photograph was taken in 1947 at Padstow in Cornwall. 12hp saloons were priced at £330 plus purchase tax of £92.8.4d while 14hp models cost £435 plus £121.11.8d purchase tax. (Author's collection)

Introduced in 1947, the MG YA/YB 1¼ litre saloon was originally proposed for 1941 had war not intervened. Artistic licence suggests this to be a much larger and faster car than it actually was. A nice machine if available, but like the greater majority of cars, they were exported. (Author's collection)

One of the most interesting of post-war designs was the Gerald Palmer-designed Jowett Javelin with its 1½ litre horizontally-opposed four-cylinder OHV engine. Features included fast-back styling, all-torsion bar suspension and rack and pinion steering. Going into production in 1947, some 23,000 Javelins were built.
(Author's collection)

The Renault Eight was assembled at Acton with all production being exported. The design was updated from its pre-war version to include four doors instead of two. Despite the cars being unavailable in the United Kingdom, such advertisements did at least maintain the Renault name to British motorists.
(Author's collection)

Today, an export success—

TOMORROW, A HOME MARKET WINNER

Although at present the entire production of the Renault Eight is labelled "for export only", we hope in time to reserve a good slice of our output for the home market, where this economical family car is bound to find favour. The Renault Eight is a genuine post-war car, not a "utility" adaptation of a pre-war model. In it the Renault tradition of strength, reliability and low running costs has been maintained and many new features added, bringing it into line with the latest ideas in automobile design. The power-weight ratio has been studied closely, with the result that there is more room and comfort for passengers and a better turn of speed than one would expect from a car of only eight horse-power. Four-wheel, hydraulic brakes make for greater control and ease of handling. Keep a lookout for the name Renault; it is going to play a big part in the progress of post-war motoring.

NOTE THESE REFINEMENTS

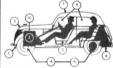

1. Independent front wheel springing and powerful double action shock absorbers.
2. Powerful 3-bearing crankshaft 8 h.p. engine.
3. Bonnet opening in one piece giving easy access to engine, battery and tools.
4. Hydraulic brakes front and rear.
5. Adjustable front seats.
6. Scientific weight distribution for safety and comfort.
7. All metal roof panel.
8. Four wide doors for easy access.
9. Increased petrol tank capacity—8½ gallons approx.
10. Hot-spot in exhaust manifold.

RENAULT EIGHT

RENAULT LIMITED WESTERN AVENUE LONDON W.3

It was 1948 before any of the new generation Rootes models went into production. The styling of this Phase III Hillman Minx was influenced by Raymond Loewy and his work for Studebaker. The full-width styling echoed themes emanating from America, and the car sold well in the United Kingdom. (Author's collection)

You get so much more out of the Minx!

... and you get so much more into it !

Rootes introduced the Sunbeam-Talbot 90 in 1948 which was replaced by the MkII in 1950, itself supplanted by the MkIIA in 1952. Produced as a saloon and sports convertible coupé, it is the MkII that is depicted here, its top speed of 86mph being appreciated by a sporting clientele. The car's interior was most attractive and well-equipped, and the manufacturer maximised on the model's success in winning the 1948, 1949 and 1950 International Alpine Trials. (Author's collection)

SUNBEAM-TALBOT 90

Austerity in the USA brought about the Crosley, a utilitarian small car that was produced in a range of body styles to include saloons, station wagons, convertibles, vans and pick-ups. Fuel economy was an important factor on these cars, with 50mpg being possible. (Author's collection)

Exporting cars was not confined to the United Kingdom. Here, the first Beetle to be exported to the USA is being loaded aboard a vessel in 1949 prior to its transatlantic journey. On the left is Ben Pon who did much to sell the VW to world markets. (Volkswagen)

Left: This evocative advertisement for the Sunbeam Alpine makes no apologies for creating a distinct image that relies heavily on artistic licence. Note the length of the bonnet compared with the cockpit and size of the occupants. (Author's collection)

Right: Citroën also exported large numbers of vehicles from its Slough factory with many cars destined for the British Commonwealth, however, from 1946 some were made available for the home market. The four-cylinder and six-cylinder saloons remained in production until 1955, although French production continued until 1957. The 'basic' refers to the basic petrol ration. (Author's collection)

Italy's charming Little Mouse, the Fiat Topolino, sold in large numbers before the war, and in post-war years served as a reliable yet inexpensive transport for countless Europeans. In France it was badged as the Simca Cinq and it also found a ready market in Britain. The 500B Belvedere station wagon afforded much more in the way of accommodation than the saloon. (Author's collection)

The French were happy to drive around in the tiny Biscooter, while the Spanish favoured the Biscuter. The cars were the same and were developed by Gabriel Voisin (1880-1973), one of the finest automotive and aeronautical engineers. The French had a love affair with tiny cars that were frugal to run, many of which now command cult status. (National Motor Museum)

Post-war, Fiat updated the Topolino, this being the 500C. In a period of austerity its frugal fuel consumption proved to be a major benefit, making the most of meagre petrol rations. The Topolino was a two-seater, the manufacturer encouraging the use of cushions on the floor of the rear compartment on which to seat young children. (Maria Cairnie)

Austerity Motoring from Armistice until the mid-Fifties

The diminutive size of the Bond Minicar can be judged from this photograph, taken in Devon in the late 1940s. Despite their fragile appearance, Bonds were capable of achieving long distances in relative comfort.
(Author's collection)

A lot of interest is being shown in this Bond Minicar which was pictured in Huddersfield between 1948 and 1949. These lightweight three-wheelers, powered by 197cc twin-stroke engines with integral gearboxes installed above the steering assembly, relied on tyre pressures for rear suspension.
(Graham Hull)

EASY TO DRIVE! EASY TO START! EASY TO PARK! EASY TO PAY FOR! .. THE Gordon COSTS LESS FOR EVERYTHING!

PARKING . . . One of the greatest worries of the motorist to-day is parking. No matter how busy the main thoroughfare the " Gordon " with its overall length of only 10 ft. 2 ins. and the greater steering lock of the 3-wheeler, is sure to find a spot in which to park.

BRAKING . . . In these days of speed and quick decisions the " Gordon's " independent braking on all three wheels gives the driver every confidence in his ability to brake instantly and safely, particularly on steep and dangerous hills.

TRAFFIC . . . Easy manoeuverability in all its gears, including reverse, makes the " Gordon " a very easy car to effect a quick getaway, whilst crowded streets hold less difficulties for the " Gordon " with its width of only 4 ft. 9½ ins.

CRUISING . . . For comfort, smooth running and road holding the " Gordon " is unequalled for a car of its size. Its powerful 197 c.c. engine is especially tuned to cruise at 40 miles per hour.

When it came to design and running costs, nothing could beat the Gordon for economy. Chain driven, the vehicle was propelled by a feeble two-stroke engine on its off-side which was a little too close to the driver's seat for comfort. The Gordon, like a number of other economy cars, was a means of transport for many families who otherwise would not have enjoyed this freedom. (Author's collection)

Reliants were popular in the early 1950s, this Regal model being part of a contrived publicity photograph. Three-wheelers were economical to run and could be driven by holders of motorcycle licences; there was also one less tyre to worry about! (Author's collection)

The Mark C Bond afforded transport for a family of four. Not entirely evident from this photograph is that the two rear seats are side facing and are only sufficient to accommodate small children. (Author's collection)

The A.C. Petite differed from other three-wheelers by the fact that it was, by comparison, luxuriously appointed and was fitted with car-like controls. It offered minimal fuel consumption from its rear-mounted 353cc twin-stroke engine. (National Motor Museum)

Why get wet?

At last! The CABIN SCOOTER is the answer to all those 'rainy day' problems. You will travel in warmth, comfort and safety both for business and pleasure. Such manoeuvrability enables easy parking, and petrol — you'd hardly notice — at 85 miles per gallon.

Standard Model . . . . £276-6-2 plus £66-12-8 P.T.
De Luxe Model . . . . £295-18-1 plus £71-6-3 P.T.

H.P. arrangements available at your dealers.

CABIN SCOOTERS LTD.
SOLE CONCESSIONAIRES IN THE UNITED KINGDOM
17 GREAT CUMBERLAND PLACE, LONDON, W.1

NOVEMBER, 1956   63

Why get wet? This was the message to motorcyclists who could benefit from car-like accommodation. Sitting in tandem, the Messerschmitt's occupants were enclosed beneath a transparent hood that hinged open to allow entry to and from the cabin. What is not said is that the interior of the vehicle became intolerably hot and claustrophobic in warm weather. This advertisement dates from 1956, although production of the Cabin Scooter began in 1953. (Author's collection)

There is only one way to get in and out of a Messerschmitt. These tiny cars were once a familiar sight in early post-war Europe and enjoyed a popular following in Britain. (Author's collection)

Above and right: Not many customers chose the Rodley as their new car for it was utilitarian in the extreme. Not only that, it experienced an unfortunate setback when examples were suddenly engulfed in flames owing to the overheating and positioning of the exhaust pipe. Rodleys cannot claim to have aesthetic styling either, as the austere lines were yet another minus point in its popularity. (Author's collection)

Deliveries of Vauxhall's first all-new post-war car commenced in 1951. The styling was obviously derived from Chevrolet. Middlesbrough Police had just taken delivery of the vehicle, along with the Bedford OB Black Maria and the Velox. (Vauxhall)

I thought, somehow, you'd have a Wolseley...

The Wolseley Owner mentions his car with a certain satisfaction for discrimination in such matters proclaims taste as well as judgment. Wolseley prestige, a legacy of fifty years of brilliant achievement, is reflected in the performance, luxury and distinction of the Six-Eighty and Four-Fortyfour, two outstanding cars in the English fine-car tradition.

The Wolseley Four-Fortyfour
4 cyl. 1,250 c.c. engine. Seating within wheelbase. Distinctive Gold-Medal winning coachwork. English leather upholstery. Controllable inbuilt ventilation system. Independent front suspension.

The Wolseley Six-Eighty
6 cyl. 2,224 c.c. engine. Exceptional Wolseley finish with polished walnut facia and window trim. Leather and Dunlopillo upholstery. Full 5-seater. Interior twin lights. Extra large luggage capacity.

Buy wisely – buy

WOLSELEY

WOLSELEY MOTORS LTD., COWLEY, OXFORD.
London Showrooms: 12, Berkeley Street, W.1.
Overseas Business : Nuffield Exports Ltd., Oxford and 41, Piccadilly, London, W.1.

SERVICE IN EUROPE
Qualified Wolseley owners planning a Continental Tour are invited to see their Wolseley dealer for details of a free service to save foreign currency.

Wolseley models are fitted with safety glass all round.

Advertisements such as this were well-placed in *Country Life* and *The Field* and were aimed at a specific clientele. When this appeared, the British Motor Corporation had already been established, bringing together the Austin, Morris, Wolseley, Riley and MG marques. (Author's collection)

A number of foreign manufacturers found favour with British customers, not least Renault's small rear-engined 4CV saloon. Photographed on Plymouth Hoe, this Acton-built 750 is competing in the 1954 Plymouth Presidential Rally. (Author's collection)

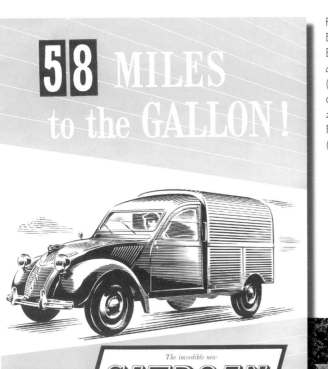

Few cars were more economical than the ultra-utilitarian British-built 2CV, depicted here in its commercial form. Even at 58mpg, the car attracted few customers who were dismayed by its obvious austerity that included barely clad (but wonderfully comfortable) tubular seats and the absence of instrumentation. Many buyers were also put off by its £565 price tag, as they could acquire an Austin A30, Ford Popular and Anglia, Morris Minor and Standard Eight for less. (Author's collection)

The Ford Consul was built from 1950 until 1956 and more than 227,000 examples were sold. The Consul heralded the introduction of larger models, including saloons and estate cars. (Ford)

The Zodiac arrived at the end of the period covered by this book. Faster than the Ford Zephyr, the car sported white wall tyres, two-tone paint and several extras including spot/ fog lamps. (Ford)

The Ford Zephyr was basically a Consul but with a six-cylinder 2262cc engine. Zephyrs could be tuned to provide a high top speed and fine acceleration, all of which were let down by uninspiring handling. (Ford)

This page and top of next page: The camper van provided a leisurely means of travel without the expense of costly hotels or trying to find suitable bed and breakfast lodgings. Among the most popular motor homes was the Volkswagen, seen here in various conversions to include the Canterbury Moto-Caravan, Pitt, and Moortown. (Author's collection)

For some motorists, owning a caravan had greater appeal than driving a motor home. Caravanning increased in popularity after the war and afforded the means of taking holidays without the expense of hotels. This Ambassador caravan is being towed by a Standard Vanguard and was pictured in the Cotswolds in 1949. (Author's collection)

Luxury and Speed in Austerity

While most people could only dream about buying cars in times of austerity, there remained a select few who were able to afford the best the motor industry could offer. Rolls-Royce, for example, sold all the cars it could produce, though the Bentley marque was deemed a lot less ostentatious.

While most Bentley customers were happy to specify standard pressed steel bodywork, an exclusive clientele insisted on their motorcars having coachwork hand-built by bespoke coachbuilders. At the time when a 'basic'

During the early 1950s cars such as this W.O.Bentley-designed Lagonda could be purchased cheaply on account of their size and fuel consumption. Lucky are those motorists who bought these cars as they are now valuable collectors' items. (National Motor Museum)

Between the wars Alvis built a formidable reputation for itself in motor sport and attracted a discerning clientele. In 1946 the TA14 sports saloon was introduced, which was essentially a pre-war design. More expensive than Rovers, the Alvis competed with Armstrong Siddeley and Lea-Francis. (Author's collection)

Bentley Mark VI cost £4038, a coachbuilt car would command nearly £5500, the price difference buying a Jaguar 3 litre with nearly enough left over to buy an 8hp Ford Anglia.

When nothing but the finest workmanship would do, the Rolls-Royce Silver Wraith was the preserve of the most discerning customer. Coachbuilt in the finest tradition, these cars were rarely owner-driven. Chauffeurs were employed to spirit their charges with grace and sophisticated silence, begging the question - what petrol crisis? The most select cars to wear the famous R-R monogram were the Phantoms, enormous in every respect and reserved exclusively for royalty and heads of state.

Daimler, too, was the epitome of unashamed luxury, the preference of royalty and choice of nobility and aristocracy. With their straight-eight engines guzzling precious pints of petrol with alacrity, they were very much part of the establishment. Smaller Daimlers were no less austere; owning one was a symbol of success.

Luxury motoring was not confined to a handful of models. Austin unveiled the Sheerline and Vanden Plas Princess in 1947, cars that arguably rivalled Bentley. Rootes' luxury Humbers, Super Snipes and Imperials, were the choice of government ministers and a familiar sight in Whitehall. Jaguars were highly regarded by successful business people seeking cars that encompassed quality and luxury. They also appealed to the sporting fraternity which rallied them with aplomb, and when that most classic of Jaguars, the XK120 with its potential speed of 120mph, went into production in 1949, most were destined for America. No one was more successful at the wheel of an XK120 than Ian and Pat Appleyard, Pat being William Lyons' daughter. Together they won the Alpine Rally in 1950, 1951 and 1952.

Luxury motoring was as much a matter of perception

Daimler realised there was an opportunity to associate its cars with the fine engineering that went into building Britain's fighting machines during the war effort. This relied heavily on the familiarity of the car's famous fluted radiator shell for advertising purposes. (Author's collection)

as it was affordable. First post-war Rovers had 1930s styling, but when the new 75, with its hint of Americanism, arrived in time for the 1949 model year, it bit at Bentley's heels.

The razor-edged styling of Triumph's Renown was also emerging as a popular choice for the discerning customer, while MG continued to produce traditional sports cars under the guise of the TC, TD and TF models. From 1947 the MG Y-Series saloons oozed

The same wartime theme is conveyed in this 1945 advertisement, which shows the Daimler still wearing its black-out apparel. (Author's collection)

Men who design finer and faster machines choose this car for their own use

Daimler

THE DAIMLER COMPANY LIMITED · LONDON AND COVENTRY

'A Car Far Ahead Of Its Time' is the Daimler theme, with this July 1945

A CAR FAR AHEAD OF ITS TIME

By 1930 Daimler had perfected the fluid flywheel, the famous oil drive. At once it gave an ease and smoothness of control which were startling. The whole aspect of car driving was changed. *Now America follows Daimler's example.* All their newest leading models will be fitted with fluid drive. And so of course will your new Daimler be.

THE DAIMLER COMPANY LIMITED · LONDON AND COVENTRY

BY APPOINTMENT

Daimler

advertisement departing from the association with war. Anticipating selling the majority of its output abroad, Daimler establishes links with the American market. (Author's collection)

pre-war styling which remained until the Magnette appeared in 1953, this being the companion to the equivalent Riley Pathfinder and Wolseley models.

Low volume specialist manufacturers, such as Allard, Alvis, Armstrong Siddeley, Aston Martin, Bristol, Healey, Jensen and Lagonda, catered for a select and discerning clientele which demanded quality with performance.

Flying in the face of austerity, speed was a requirement that the motor industry met with some success. When the exquisite Bentley R-Type Continental was introduced in 1952, it was the fastest and most expensive production saloon in the British catalogue. Far more adventurous was Rover's experimental gas turbine car, Jet 1, a hugely modified 75 that went to work on Belgium's Jabbeke Highway in June 1952 to achieve speeds in excess of 150mph. Austin, too, dabbled with gas turbine technology using the Sheerline as an experimental vehicle. Austin's endeavours were not nearly as successful as Rover's.

Motor sport successfully promoted a motor industry fighting to return to normality. The Monte Carlo Rally attracted some of the best known drivers including Mike Couper, Sydney Allard, Reg Parnell, Sheila Van Damm, Tommy and Elsie Wisdom, Denis Jenkinson, Stirling Moss and Mike Hawthorn. When the British Grand Prix was held at Silverstone in 1950 all hopes were pinned on the new BRM being successful, but were disappointed.

Relieving the stress of war, nothing could revive hope and expectations more than John Cobb's world record landspeed attempt with the Railton-Mobil Special at Bonneville in 1947. It was mid-September when Cobb began trials which resulted in him achieving 415mph to establish a new record of 394.2mph for the two-way average speed. The achievement was not only good for national morale, but was a feat for British engineering and technology.

Above and below: Jaguar began its post-war production in 1945 with 1½, 2½ and 3½ litre models, the four-cylinder 1½ litre car being illustrated here. All three versions shared similar styling which originated in the 1930s and displayed the most inviting interiors with their large, comfortable and softly upholstered seats. (Author's collection)

Armstrong Siddeley made no bones about naming its post-war cars Lancaster and Hurricane after types of aircraft synonymous with the RAF and Britain's victory over Germany. In 1949 Armstrong Siddeley introduced the Whitley, thus naming it after yet another successful aeroplane. (Author's collection)

Pictured outside of the firm's Solihull works in December 1945, these Rover Ten saloons were the first vehicles to leave the shadow factory following its transfer to car production. Rover customers were mainly professional people who wanted quality combined with sporting appeal. (LAT Photographic)

ROVER

ONE OF BRITAIN'S FINE CARS — NOW MADE FINER

For 1948 and 1949, Rover built the four-cylinder 60 and six-cylinder 75 models, the styling of which showed its 1930's ancestry. These were well-appointed vehicles, the specification including choice hide upholstery with the driver's seat being adjustable for height as well as leg room. (Author's collection)

Rolls-Royce's Crewe factory was also given over to car production at the end of the war, and a line of Bentley Mk VIs undergoing final preparation can be seen here. Despite austerity, the demand for these cars was keen, both at home and abroad. The Bentley marque was being more vigorously marketed than Rolls-Royce in view of the latter being hardly compatible with ration books. (Rolls-Royce)

When Austin introduced the Sheerline, the company hoped to attract customers who might otherwise have chosen a Bentley. The car's styling was certainly a plus point, along with enormous Lucas P100 headlamps and plenty of wood and leather that exuded luxury, all at the relatively affordable price of £1277. The car illustrated here is one of three prototypes. (Author's collection)

At the same time as the Sheerline was introduced, Austin announced the 4 litre Princess with Vanden Plas coachwork. There were some styling changes including headlamps that were faired into the wings, and luxury extended to pull-down picnic tables housed in the front seat squabs. At £2218 the Princess undercut Bentley's price by £1820. (Author's collection)

Britain's export drive persuaded Rolls-Royce to undertake a 16-week coast-to-coast tour of America beginning in October 1947. The cars were exhibited in New York's Astor Gallery before embarking on a journey comprising more than 20,000 miles. The tour was under the direction of Jack Scott, Rolls-Royce's sales manager, and Captain Vautier, the firm's overseas representative. (Author's collection)

John Cobb's successful landspeed record attempt in 1947 with his Napier-Railton was a huge boost to British morale. The record-breaking car used Lockheed brakes, something the component manufacturer lost no time in advertising. (Author's collection)

THE FAMOUS NAPIER-RAILTON AGAIN

Mr. John Cobb EXCEEDS 403 m.p.h.

Sets up new record of 394·196 M.P.H.
(subject to official confirmation)

Mr. John Cobb, whose car was equipped with Lockheed Brakes, writes :—" . . on these land speed record attempts the car has to be reduced in speed from 400 m.p.h to rest in under 5 miles, and unless the brakes are very good, believe me, it would not be possible to stop in the distance."

Lockheed Leadership
AUTOMOTIVE PRODUCTS COMPANY LTD., LEAMINGTON SPA

During the first week of February 1948, Hooper coachbuilders delivered this 27hp Daimler to H.R.H. Princess Elizabeth. The car, which was fitted as a state limousine, is pictured in the Mall being driven to Buckingham Palace by two RAF personnel. Finished in black with beige upholstery, its pillarless rear compartment was fitted with two luxuries, a heater and radio. The limousine was a wedding present, paid for by members of the armed services. (LAT Photographic)

In 1949 Rolls-Royce introduced the Silver Dawn, sister-car to the Bentley Mk VI. Seen on the assembly lines at Crewe with its Bentley equivalent, these were the first Rolls-Royce and Bentley models to employ pressed-steel bodies. (Rolls-Royce)

The Silver Dawn, pictured outside the Rolls-Royce factory at Crewe, was initially available for export, and was not sold on the home market until 1952. It was identical to the Bentley Mk VI save for the radiator, badging, facia layout and carburetion. (Rolls-Royce)

Shortly after they were married, Their Royal Highnesses The Princess Elizabeth and The Duke of Edinburgh took delivery of this Rolls-Royce Phantom IV. The car was built to the order of The Duke, and when Her Majesty Queen Elizabeth II ascended the throne it was adopted as a State car in preference to the Daimler which had been a wedding present. Only eighteen Phantom IVs were built, all of which were reserved for royalty and heads of state. (Rolls-Royce)

The Rolls-Royce and Bentley showroom at Conduit Street, probably the most famous of all motorcar emporiums in the world. On display in 1951 are a Rolls-Royce Silver Wraith and two Bentley Mk VIs. The demonstration of such wealth was a paradox to an age of austerity when many people could not afford even the cheapest car, new or used. (Rolls-Royce)

This Mark V Jaguar is negotiating a tight corner at speed during the Monte Carlo Rally in 1951. Driven by Messrs W.H. Waring and W.H. Wadham, the car started from Glasgow and was placed ninth in the general classification. In 1950 the car would have cost £1247 - nearly the price of a small and modest new house. (Douglas Sharp)

In this 1951 advertisement for the Humber Super Snipe the artist has outrageously exaggerated the car's lines. Humber was Rootes' most prestigious marque and the background scenery gives the impression of great affluence. (Author's collection)

Bristol cars are highly revered and sought after, not least the beautifully styled 400 which helped earn foreign currency for Britain when it was most needed. The bidding was strong when this surviving example, dating from 1949, came under the auctioneer's hammer. (Author's collection)

The De Havilland Comet and the Bentley Continental were symbols of prosperity. The Comet entered service in 1952 and was the world's first commercial jet airliner while the Bentley Continental was the fastest and most expensive production car. (Rolls-Royce)

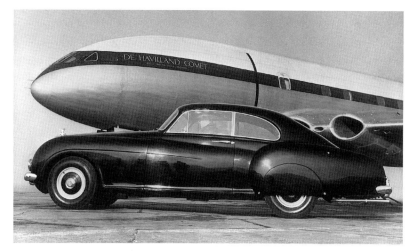

This 1946 Slough Citroën Light Fifteen checks in at a control point while participating in the London Motor Club's London Rally in September 1952. Note the fashions, and the marshals' military uniforms. (Author's collection)

The development of Rover's gas turbine car was another morale boosting event in the shadow of the war years. At the wheel of JET 1 is Spen King, the engineer responsible for the gas turbine project at Rover. He took the car to Belgium where speed tests were carried out on the then newly opened Jabbeke Highway. He piloted the car with Peter Wilks above 152mph, no mean achievement in 1952. (BMIHT)

The car
in
front
is of course
the dashing Daimler
CONQUEST

The dashing Daimler Conquest inspired the dream of speed and comfort for many motorists who could barely afford one of Britain's cheaper cars. It was attractively priced at a little over £1500, especially when a new Rover 75 cost nearly £1300. (Author's collection)

This view of the 1952 London Motor Show epitomises luxury in austerity with the 1953 models shown. Famous names such as Armstrong Siddeley, Lanchester and Lea-Francis are evident, many of which have now fallen by the wayside. The Chevrolets make for an interesting comparison with the styling of the Rolls-Royce models. (Rolls-Royce)

This Rolls-Royce Silver Dawn is being carefully loaded aboard the Empress of Australia, another export sale to earn money for Britain. (SHRMF)

Entering the Monte Carlo Rally was an excellent way for manufacturers to publicise their cars. However, in this instance it is the Metropolitan Police of 1956 which is promoting its image. Accompanied by their senior officer, drivers Shillabeer, Carruthers and Taylor are posing alongside their 1954 Humber Super Snipe before embarking on their rally attempt. (Metropolitan Police)

'One of Britain's fine cars' outside a stately home makes for an impressive advertisement. The two examples of publicity material shown on this page illustrate that Rover's marketing approach was firmly aimed towards the professional classes and aristocracy. The artwork is particularly appealing, and a number of similarly evocative renderings graced the company's catalogues during the 1950s. (Author's collection)

Often referred to as 'The poor man's Bentley', Rovers were marketed as 'One of Britain's fine cars'. They were the choice of doctors and dentists, bankers, solicitors and gentlemen farmers, and they possessed that essential presence which made them stand apart from other vehicles. Illustrated here is an impression of the Rover 60. (Author's collection)

Photographed in Belgrave Square in 1954, this Rolls-Royce Phantom IV belonged to the late Princess Margaret. Parked in the distance is a small Standard saloon, ahead of which is a Bedford van. An Austin FX3 taxicab is about to pass a waiting Bentley, while opposite the camera is a Volkswagen Beetle and, alongside it, another Standard. (Rolls-Royce)

Conveying an impression of wealth, this Mulliner-bodied Bentley Mk VI makes a fine picture amid regal surroundings. This car would have cost well in excess of £6000, more than most people would have paid for a more than modest home in 1952. (Rolls-Royce)

By the mid-1950s Britain was emerging from austerity. Cars and luxury goods were becoming all the more affordable and there was a sense of greater prosperity within the country. Cars like these, pictured inside the Conduit Street showrooms of Rolls-Royce and Bentley, were, nevertheless, beyond the pockets of all but the most affluent people. (Rolls-Royce)

The Cenotaph as pictured in 1956. A sign of austerity is the Austin FX3 taxicab while the Wolseley 6/90 suggests increasing prosperity. The photograph is particularly poignant as it leads us to remember those who died in conflict. (Metropolitan Police).

British Police Cars
Nick Walker

A nostalgic and heavily illustrated look at the cars used by the British Police from the very earliest days until the end of the 1970s. Throughout the book it's the cars that are the stars, from the Edwardian Humber to comparatively modern Rovers and Granadas of the seventies.

Motor Racing at Goodwood in the Sixties
Tony Gardiner

Tony Gardiner was a regular spectator at Goodwood before the popular Sussex track's forced closure in 1966. His fascinating photos remind us of an era of motor racing very different from today's, and illustrate an amazing variety of machinery from Lotus Cortinas to the Essex Racing team's Aston Martin Zagatos.

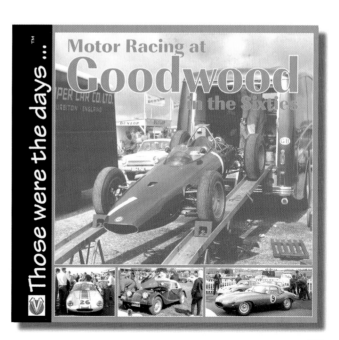

Other titles in this series

The Dune Buggy Phenomenon
James Hale

The dune buggy has been an international phenomenon during the decades since the 1960s. For the first time, in words and stunning photographs, this is the full story of the Buggy. This superb volume contains many rare and archive pictures, and will become a bible for enthusiasts of these fun cars.

Three Wheelers
Malcolm Bobbitt

Three wheelers have played an intrisic part in the history of the motor vehicle, from Aero Morgans to Coventry Victor, BSA and Reliant. Three wheelers had their place in motor sport as well as providing essential transport for thousands of families. A nostalgic look in the rearview mirror at the fascinating and often weird world of the three wheeled car.

Index

Abell, Major George 29
AC 51, 64
AEC 14
Air Ministry 7
Allard 74
Allard, Sydney 74
Alvis 72
Ambulances 14, 15, 25
Appleyard, John 73
Appleyard, Pat 73
Armstrong Siddeley 8, 32, 48, 72, 74, 75, 87
Aston Martin 74
Austin Motor Co. Ltd 7, 8, 11, 14, 16, 25, 31 42, 43, 47, 52, 67, 73, 74, 77, 78
Austin, Herbert (later Lord Austin) 8, 47
Austin models
    8hp 47
    10hp 47
    12hp 47
    16hp 47
    A30 47
    A90 Atlantic 48
    K2 Ambulance 14, 25
    Eight 14
    Princess 73, 78
    Seven 36
    Sheerline 73, 74, 77, 78
    Ten 25
Auxiliary Fire Service 10

Bedford 74
Bentley 31, 32, 52, 72-74, 77, 81, 83, 85, 90, 91
Bentley, W.O. 72
Biscooter 61
Biscuter 61
Blackout regulations 9-13, 16
BMW 7, 29
Bond 51, 62, 64
Bristol Aeroplane Co 7, 8, 21, 29
Bristol Brabazon 29
Bristol Cars 21, 29, 31, 74, 84
British Motor Corporation 67
British School of Motoring 26
BRM 74
Bubblecars 51, 64, 65
Bury Felt 38

Camper vans 70, 71
Canadian Military Pattern vehicles 8
Car Collection Co 26
Car radios 40
Chevrolet 49, 66, 87
Citroën 6, 8, 35, 41, 50, 51, 59, 68, 85
Cobb, John 74, 79

Comet jet airliner 85
Corroid enamel paint 34, 40
Couper, Mike 41, 74
Cripps, Sir Stafford 21-23
Crosley 58

Daimler 7, 73, 74, 80, 86
Dalton, Hugh 23
De Havilland 85
Dormobile 32
Dowding, Sir Hugh 7
Duke of Edinburgh 82
Duranide 34

Fedden, Roy 7, 21, 22
Fiat 21, 35, 60, 61
Ford, Henry 51, 52
Ford (inc Ford Motor Co) 5, 6, 8, 19, 20, 27, 28, 30, 49, 53
    Anglia 8, 27-29, 73
    Consul 68, 69
    Popular 30
    Prefect 27, 28, 30, 49
    V8 Pilot 28, 49
    Y 5, 6
    Zephyr 69
    Zodiac 69

Girling 38
Gordon 51, 63
Greifzu, Paul 7
Grey-Green Coaches 46
Grundy's Petroids 33
Guy Motors 13

Harold Radford Ltd 32
Hawthorn, Mike 74
Healey 74
Healey, Donald 47
Henley Tyres 33, 34
Hillman 8, 11, 26, 31, 45, 49, 57
Hirst, Major Ivan 53
Hitler, Adolf 5
Home Guard 15
Hooper coachwork 80
Humber 26, 31, 32, 49, 54, 73, 84, 88

Issigonis, Alec 24, 49

Jaguar 31, 32, 73, 75, 83
Jeep 32, 42
Jenkinson, Denis 74
Jensen 74
Jowett 50, 56

Kendall, William 21
King George VI 9
King, Spen 86

Lagonda 72, 74
Lanchester 47, 87
Land Rover 32, 42
Lea-Francis 72, 87
Lockheed 79
Loewy, Raymond 49, 57
Lord, Leonard 47
Lyons, William 73

Martin Walter Ltd 32
Messerschmitt 51, 64, 65
Metropolitan Police 11, 45, 88
MG 25, 55, 67, 73, 74
Middlesbrough Police 66
Ministry of Home Security 16
Ministry of Supply 22, 34
Ministry of Transport 35
Monte Carlo Rally 41, 50, 74, 83, 88
Morris Commercial 10
Morris (inc. Morris Motors) 6, 10, 14, 15, 24-26, 31, 42, 49, 50, 67
    Minor 24-26, 49
    Mosquito 24
    Ten 22, 47, 50
Morris, William (see also Lord Nuffield) 22
Moss, Stirling 74
Mulliner coachwork 91

Napier 8
Napier-Railton 79
Nuffield, Lord 49
Nuffield Organisation 22, 25

Palestine Motors 23
Palmer, Gerald 50, 56
Parnell, Reg 74
Petrol rationing 5-6, 8-11, 14, 17, 18
Plus-Gas 33
Plymouth 51
Pon, Ben 58
Princess Elizabeth 80, 82
Princess Margaret 90

Queen Elizabeth 9
Queen Elizabeth II 82

Radclyfe, Major Charles 53
Railton-Mobil 74
R.E.A.L coachbuilders 16
Redex 33
Reliant 51, 63
Renault 8, 51, 56, 67
Rexine 34
Riley 24, 31, 47, 52, 67, 74

Rodley 65
Rolls-Royce 3, 8, 15, 32, 72, 73, 77, 79, 81-83, 87, 88, 90, 91
Rootes Group 7, 26, 49, 57, 73, 84
Rover 7, 8, 21, 31, 42, 49, 72-74, 76, 86, 89

Scott, Jack 79
Seaman, Richard 7
Scammell Scarab 46
Shadow factories 3, 7-9, 20, 76
Simca 60
Singer 8, 49
Society of Motor Manufacturers & Traders (SMMT) 21-23, 47
Speed limits 9, 13
Standard 8, 23, 31, 42, 51, 71, 90
Strauss, George 23
Studebaker 49, 57
Suez Crisis 6, 23, 51
Sunbeam 49
Sunbeam Alpine 59
Sunbeam Talbot 49, 57, 59

Tank production 14
Taxicabs 10, 11, 20, 43, 90, 92
Tecalemit 37
Three wheelers 51, 62-65
Touring coachwork 31
Tyres 10, 33, 34
Tyresoles 34
Triumph 73

Utilecon 32

Van Damm, Sheila 74
Valay 34
Vanden Plas 73
Vautier, Capt. 79
Vauxhall 39, 49, 51, 55, 66
    Velox 49, 66
    Wyvern 49
Voisin, Gabriel 61
Volkswagen 22, 51-53, 58, 70, 71, 90
Vol-o-pep 32, 33

Wadham, W.H. 83
Waring, W.H. 83
West Yorkshire Constabulary 13
White, George 29
Wilks, Maurice 32, 42
Wilks, Peter 86
Wisdom, Elsie 74
Wisdom, Tommy 74
Wolseley 11, 35, 43, 45, 47, 49, 67, 74, 92

Visit Veloce on the web - www.veloce.co.uk